Also by Colin O'Brady

The Impossible First

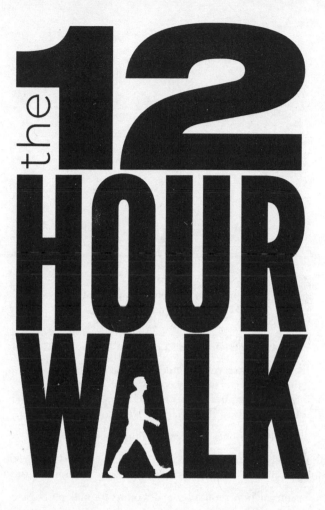

THE 12 HOUR WALK

INVEST ONE DAY, CONQUER YOUR MIND,
AND UNLOCK YOUR BEST LIFE

COLIN O'BRADY

SCRIBNER

NEW YORK   LONDON   TORONTO   SYDNEY   NEW DELHI

Scribner
An Imprint of Simon & Schuster, Inc.
1230 Avenue of the Americas
New York, NY 10020

First Scribner hardcover edition August 2022

SCRIBNER and design are registered trademarks of The Gale Group, Inc.,
used under license by Simon & Schuster, Inc., the publisher of this work.

For information about special discounts for bulk purchases,
please contact Simon & Schuster Special Sales at 1-866-506-1949
or business@simonandschuster.com.

The Simon & Schuster Speakers Bureau can bring authors
to your live event. For more information or to book an event,
contact the Simon & Schuster Speakers Bureau at 1-866-248-3049
or visit our website at www.simonspeakers.com.

Interior design by Michelle Marchese

Manufactured in the United States of America

1   3   5   7   9   10   8   6   4   2

Library of Congress Cataloging-in-Publication Data has been applied for.

ISBN 978-1-9821-3316-0
ISBN 978-1-9821-3318-4 (ebook)

IN MEMORY OF

JP, Ali, John, Atanas, Sergi, Antonios, and Dixie

Thank you for always singing your songs.

You are all forever alive in my heart.

I only went out for a walk and finally concluded to stay out till sundown, for going out, I found, was really going in.

—JOHN MUIR

CONTENTS

PART I

INTRODUCTION

Pos·si·ble Mind·set *noun*

\ ˈpä-sə-bəl-ˈmīn(d)-ˌset \

an empowered way of thinking that
unlocks a life of limitless possibilities.

1

WHAT'S YOUR EVEREST?

> The mass of men lead lives of quiet desperation.
>
> —HENRY DAVID THOREAU

What if I told you I'd found a way to help you live a more fulfilling life?

What if I could send you on a journey that would leave you feeling like you can accomplish just about anything—that would teach you how to shed the limiting beliefs that are holding you back, and instead unlock your best life?

Here's the best part—what if you could complete that journey in just a single day?

▲ ▲ ▲

My heart raced and I struggled to breathe.

Moments before, a confident strength had propelled me toward the summit slopes of Mount Everest, but in an instant everything had changed, shattering my calm demeanor.

I was now fighting for my life.

Blue sky turned to ominous gray, and what had been a gentle breeze became thunderous gusts of fifty-mile-per-hour wind, nearly blowing me off my feet. The snow whipping around my face stung the exposed sections of my skin like a thousand tiny needles. I couldn't feel my fingers or my toes as the windchill plummeted below negative sixty degrees.

Gripped by fear, I found each step hard-earned. I stumbled through the "Death Zone," an area above 26,000 feet that owed its notorious nickname to the fact that, at such an altitude, the human body slowly dies.

"Wait . . . did you see any dead bodies on Everest?" a gray-haired man asked me from the corner of the room.

As I continued to share my stories of adventure, more and more questions came flying at me.

"How did you go to the bathroom when it was minus-thirty degrees in Antarctica?"

"Forty-foot swells, in a twenty-eight-foot rowboat? How do you survive that?"

The questions were coming at me, left and right—questions I'd heard before, but *this* time they were being asked by a group of enormously successful men—hedge fund managers, industrial tycoons, and billionaire investors. Unlike the mostly younger or middle-aged folks who pepper me with questions after my keynote addresses and other public appearances, these men had reached an age where the roads defining their life's journey— avenues paved in gold—tended to be in the rearview mirror.

We were seated around a dining room table in a glamorous

penthouse apartment on Manhattan's Upper East Side. I was in town to speak to several hundred Wall Street executives about mindset, taking risks, and overcoming obstacles, and I'd been invited here on the eve of my speech to visit with a select group of them—CEOs mostly— in a more intimate setting.

A few minutes earlier, it had been uncertain that I'd even make it into this room.

▲ ▲ ▲

I was running a few minutes late as I hastily stepped into the building's opulent lobby and searched for the elevator.

Over my shoulder I heard a firm voice, "Where do you think *you're* going?"

"I'm headed up to the penthouse," I explained to the door-man who'd suddenly appeared behind the lobby desk.

"Um, no you're not."

"I'm expected," I said. "For a dinner party."

The guy checked me out again. I was wearing jeans, low-top Jordan sneakers, and a black T-shirt—not the dress-for-success attire he was used to seeing. He pulled a slip of paper from his pocket and studied it carefully—some kind of guest list, I imagined. Then he shook his head in that satisfied way, thinking he'd confirmed his original impression. "Look, son, if you're with catering, you need to use the service elevator."

"Maybe you can call upstairs," I suggested.

Begrudgingly, the doorman picked up the phone and mumbled something I couldn't quite hear. Then he hung up and said,

"You have a nice evening, sir." With a wave of his hand, he motioned me toward the elevators at the far end of the lobby.

I certainly hadn't expected my hosts to roll out the red carpet, but neither did I think I'd have to jump through hoops just to be allowed upstairs. I'll admit, my confidence was a bit shaken as I stepped into the elevator. It was one of those crazy-fancy Manhattan buildings where the elevator opened directly into the apartment—in this case, a palatial home with breathtaking views of the city, overlooking Central Park.

Once out of the elevator, I stepped into a room in which seven or eight men mingled over drinks. They were impeccably groomed, dressed in custom-tailored suits, and—I couldn't help but notice—some wore watches worth more than it had cost to fund my last expedition. One gentleman approached me almost immediately and introduced himself as my host.

"So glad you could make it, Colin," he said, firmly shaking my hand. He seemed friendly, yet there was in him something of the doorman's attitude. I sensed he was questioning my choice of attire.

As I took my seat at a large oval table laid out with polished silverware, a waiter stepped over to fill my wineglass.

Our host clinked his own crystal glass, and the room fell silent as everyone settled into a chair.

"Most all of us here know each other," the host said—both to me and the rest of the group. "We've been screwing each other out of deals for forty years."

The line was followed by a wave of good-natured laughter, backslaps, and shouts of "Hear, hear!"

There followed another bit of glass-clinking from the host, and as the room quieted again, he said, "Regardless, I thought it would be a good idea if we went around the table and introduced ourselves."

One by one, each guest shared a line or two of introduction. As they spoke, I started to think that they'd arrived by way of Central Casting. They were all male, all white, all about sixty-five, all graduated from the finest schools and dripping with money.

It wasn't my usual crowd.

In fact, I'd been raised by strong-minded and independent women—my mother, my five older sisters, and my grandmother. And now I was married to *another* strong woman—my wife, Jenna Besaw—who ran our businesses and helped to organize every last detail of our projects.

With no women in sight on this evening, it felt like something important was missing.

As the introductions continued, I wondered what I'd say when I had the floor. As it happened, I'd gone to Yale, like a lot of the men who'd already spoken—and I'd even worked as a Wall Street commodities trader for a *very* brief stint after graduation. So my plan at first was to reach for common ground. But then I checked myself. Common ground? Who was I kidding? Prior to Yale, I'd been a public school kid from Portland, Oregon, raised by a blended family of hippie parents in a lower middle class part of the city. When the Yale swim coach called to recruit me, my first question was "Yale . . . where is that?"

Make no mistake, I was grateful for my education, but during my four years in New Haven I'd had to make ends meet by paint-

9

ing houses all summer and relying on grants and scholarships to afford books and tuition. Basically, I was a fish out of water at Yale (a fitting metaphor, given all that time in the pool!), and as a result, I never really felt like I belonged.

"Good to be here, everybody," I said, when it was my turn to speak. "My name's Colin, and I'm an athlete and an entrepreneur."

Okay, I thought. *That should cover it.* I settled back and waited for the conversation to quickly move on to macroeconomic policy, stock market trends, or whatever else these Wall Street titans usually chatted about.

Instead, what followed was an awkward silence, signaling that I hadn't come close to covering it.

Luckily, our host stepped in to rescue me. "Hold on a second, folks," he said. "This is Colin O'Brady, the world-famous explorer, and there's a whole lot more to his story."

I smiled sheepishly and lifted my wineglass to the group, as if in greeting, while the host talked me up.

"Colin has broken ten world records," he said. "He's explored some of the most extreme and remote corners of the planet! And lived to tell the tale!"

Our host went on in greater detail, telling the group how I'd finished the Explorers Grand Slam in world record time, consecutively summiting the tallest peak on each of the seven continents, and completing expeditions to the North and South Poles. Without pausing, he relayed how I'd pulled a 375-pound sled alone across the landmass of Antarctica to complete the world's first solo, unsupported, and fully human-powered crossing of the frozen continent. And he described my world-first crossing of the Drake Passage in a rowboat.

"And he's not just an athlete," he continued. "He's also had quite a bit of success with several business ventures, had his hand in some large-scale projects in Hollywood, is a *New York Times* bestselling author, *and* runs a nonprofit working with schoolkids. He'll tell us about all this in the keynote he's giving to our group tomorrow, but I asked him here tonight so some of us could get to know him a little more informally. He's quite a remarkable young man, as you will all soon learn. And he did all of this after a horrific accident when doctors told him he'd never walk normally again. That was in Thailand, right, Colin?"

Jeez, I thought, a bit embarrassed by this lengthy intro. *This guy is good.* He'd certainly done his homework, though I couldn't help but laugh inside at his comment about my age. I was, after all, much closer to middle age than to some snot-nosed recent college grad. But to this group, I guess, I was still very much a "young man."

I nodded and said, "Yep, Thailand. I've never been more afraid."

When the host was finished with his drumroll, his guests, rather than returning to their financial conversations as I'd half-expected, turned their full attention toward me and started peppering me with questions.

"Look," I said, trying to answer that question about the dead bodies on Mount Everest. "Everest is a dangerous place. I was fortunate to still make it to the summit after surviving that unexpected storm, but the day I reached the top three people died. I

11

wasn't climbing with them. I didn't know them personally. But they all died doing what I was doing, on the same day I was doing it."

I paused—not to let the moment sink in or give it any more weight than it had on its own, but to gather my emotions. Even after four years, I couldn't tell the story of my first Everest ascent without reliving the intensity of what I'd been through.

"It's hard," I finally said. "You're staring death in the face. It's clear what the stakes are, what can happen. But it's in those moments that I feel most alive."

The men around the table knew those moments. Maybe not life-and-death moments, but moments when everything is on the line. When shit gets real.

"So how'd you get *into* this life of adventure?" was the next question fired at me.

"It was always my dream to climb Everest," I said. "Since I was a kid. I never knew how I would get there, but once I reached that summit, my desire to keep exploring became insatiable."

In instances like this, I relished the opportunity to turn the tables and ask the group one of *my* favorite questions.

"I find childhood dreams are so telling. I've been fortunate to fulfill many of mine. I imagine most of you have as well. Tell me, what was your childhood dream? What's *your* Everest?"

I sat back and waited for a flurry of responses, but I got back . . . nothing.

As I scanned the room, the guests all seemed to look away, careful not to make eye contact with me. For the first time all night they were reserved, taciturn, perhaps even shy. I was shocked.

What's your Everest?

It's a question that usually invites a thought-provoking conversation about dreams fulfilled, and, yes, it sometimes ignites vulnerable remarks about dreams unrealized. On this night, however . . . crickets. So I let this line of questioning slide as these billionaires turned the tables back on me, which was what they seemed to prefer.

After the evening had run its course, and the dessert plates had been cleared, I stood to say my goodbyes. As I was about to get on the elevator to leave, I felt a hand on my arm. I looked back and saw a face I recognized from around the table, belonging to a man who'd been pretty much silent throughout the dinner. The man seemed to be a decade or so older than the other guests— maybe mid-seventies or even eighty. He was white-haired, and slender, but his eyes had this kind of rheumy look that gave him away as someone who maybe was counting the days he had left.

"Perhaps I can have a moment of your time, Colin," he said, drawing me in close, away from the others.

"Yeah, sure," I said, not quite knowing what to expect.

"I want to apologize for my friends here," he said, indicating the others. "You'd asked us a very important question, and no one seemed to want to answer. About our childhood dreams."

"There's no need to apologize," I said. "Maybe it was too personal of a question for this group."

He laughed. "For most of us, yes," he said. "For me, too, I'm afraid. But I so appreciate your time, and your perspective, that I must tell you a little something about myself. It feels important."

My curiosity was piqued.

The old man went on to tell me how when he was a kid, he used to go to a summer camp in upstate New York, where he swam and hiked and paddled around the lake in a rowboat. "There isn't a day that goes by when I don't think about being back on that rowboat," he said. He paused for a beat, and I got the feeling he was choosing his words carefully. "That question you asked us," he finally said, "'What's your Everest?' I wonder what would have happened in my life if I'd given that some thought as a younger man. If I'd actually had the gumption to go after it. What a precious gift you've given yourself, to have the courage to chase your dreams and make them come true."

"You're right about that, sir," I said. "It *is* precious. But what about you? It's never too late to ask yourself the same question."

"I'm afraid that time has come and gone for me," he said.

"No disrespect, sir," I said, "but there's no clock on our hopes and dreams."

Unwilling to leave this guy hanging beneath the weight of his unfinished thoughts, I put the question to him again. I said, "When you were a boy, when you were a younger man, what did you dream of becoming one day? What seemingly impossible goal did you think was just out of reach?"

I was stunned by this man's response. He shook his head and held out his hands, palms up—the body language of vulnerability. He said, "I honestly don't remember. I could stand here and say I wanted to play for the Yankees, or become an astronaut, and it would sound good and maybe even get close to it, but it wouldn't be the truth. For decades, I got so caught up in what I thought I *had* to do that I stopped listening to my heart."

Then he leaned in and finished his thought with a whisper. "I've made a whole lot of money in my life, Colin," he said, without an ounce of bluster. "I'm rich beyond most people's wildest dreams. But I'd trade it all for the chance to go back and maybe do things over a little differently."

I could have cried—and as I looked up, I noticed that my new friend was getting a little watery-eyed himself.

"Promise me something," the man said, as he shook my hand in parting. "Keep doing what you're doing. Keep chasing your bliss. Keep following that story inside of you."

In that moment, it wasn't clear to me what this man had lost—maybe it was the simplicity he once knew as a kid, or the stillness he'd found on that lake, or the possibility of what lay ahead. Whatever it was, despite the external appearances of having it all, he'd wanted something else out of life, something *more*, and he'd concluded that I'd somehow found what he was missing.

▲ ▲ ▲

As I rode the elevator back down to the lobby, I thought of the Thoreau quote I used to open this chapter: "The mass of men lead lives of quiet desperation." It's one of my very favorite quotes, a compelling reminder that too many of us are willing to settle—to give up on our dreams. Too many of us are held back by limiting beliefs, unable to get out of our own heads and commit to living our best lives. Thoreau's line is also one of the most *misquoted* in American literature, because a lot of people offer this version: "Most men lead lives of quiet desperation and die with their song still inside them." Thoreau never wrote that last part, but, at that precise moment, that was the phrase that rang through my head.

In many ways, the book you hold in your hands is my response to that recent wistful exchange with a regret-filled man. It's my way of fulfilling the promise he asked me to make, to keep chasing my bliss and following the story inside me. But my larger goal is to spread this message so that as many people as possible trade lives of quiet desperation for lives of deep fulfillment. I've developed a tool to help people do that . . . to help *you* do that.

Is your song still inside you? Are your dreams unfulfilled?

Climbing Mount Everest was *my* childhood dream, but you likely had—or *have*—a different dream. Tell me, what is it? What does your best life look like? It doesn't have to be an extreme test of physical strength or endurance or about a specific achievement. It can be about family, career, music, travel, happiness, contentment . . . making a million dollars or saving a million lives . . . whatever moves the needle for you, whatever's just out of reach. Where do you want to go? What do you want to accomplish? How do you want to spend your days?

This book is meant to help you answer those questions, and actually give you a tangible plan to turn those dreams into reality. After all, as author Katherine Paterson famously said, "A dream without a plan is just a wish."

Step 1: I need you to answer this question for yourself.

What's your Everest?

Allow yourself to dream, without limits—yes, set aside whatever else you've got going on, whatever limiting beliefs have held you back.

Take a moment to really think about it, then fill in the blank below:

My Everest is _____.

Hold that dream in your heart and turn the page, because I'm going to show you how to conquer your mind and unlock your best life. Summiting the mountain you're meant to climb is way closer than you think.

THE 12-HOUR WALK

Everywhere is walking distance if you have the time.

—STEVEN WRIGHT

So, real talk: Why haven't you reached the summit of your personal Mount Everest?

That song inside of you—why is it still unsung?

What's stopping you from living your best life?

My guess is you're being held back by one of the many stories you're probably telling yourself.

Your internal monologue goes something like, "I'm not living my best life because . . ."

- ▶ "I don't have enough time."
- ▶ "I don't have enough money."
- ▶ "I don't have the right friends."
- ▶ "I don't know what to do."
- ▶ "I'm afraid of failing."
- ▶ "I hate being uncomfortable."

You accept these stories as truths, but what if I told you that they were lies? Lies, excuses, defense mechanisms—call them whatever you want. Here in this book, I'm choosing to call them *limiting beliefs*. They're just that, beliefs, and beliefs can be changed, adapted, and overwritten.

You decide. You are the story you tell yourself.

In the pages that follow I'll reveal the keys to conquering your mind and authoring new stories about yourself. These keys will allow you to develop what I call a:

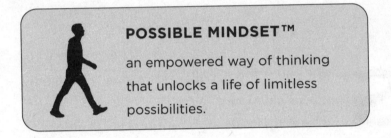

POSSIBLE MINDSET™

an empowered way of thinking that unlocks a life of limitless possibilities.

With a Possible Mindset you'll be able to reach summits, aspirations, and goals that have forever seemed out of reach. You'll be equipped with the tools to break free from what's been holding you back.

By adopting a Possible Mindset you'll soon realize that everything you've ever dreamed of is, in fact, *possible*.

A Possible Mindset is *not* something that just a select few people can possess—quite the opposite. *Everyone* has the capability to train their mind using a few simple steps that I'll teach you in this book. By the time you finish reading the last page, you'll be well on the path to achieving high levels of success and, most important, finding deep fulfillment.

The guidance I'll share isn't theoretical, it's been forged by my real-life experiences. It comes from actually having been in the arena—from failing, and falling, and getting scraped up along the way. It comes from wrestling with all of the same limiting beliefs you're dealing with but learning how to overcome them and thrive.

At its culmination this book will leave you with a single challenge, something you can accomplish in a single day . . . an experience that will open the door to living your best life immediately.

I've developed this one-day prescription to purge you of limiting beliefs and prove to you that *you* have the power to shift to a Possible Mindset to achieve anything.

But first, before I share that prescription, I'm going to tell you how I got here . . .

▲ ▲ ▲

It was May 2020, just a few months after that ritzy Manhattan dinner. The world was in lockdown—in the tight grip of a pandemic we didn't yet understand. My wife, Jenna, and I were following the stay-at-home mandate with our dog—a playful wheaten terrier named Jack—at my family's cabin on the Oregon Coast, in the town of Manzanita.

Like the lives of everyone else in the world, ours had been on hold since mid-March. I'd just published my first book, only to find my book tour cut short. My keynote speaking engagements were canceled. My next expedition? Also canceled.

It was a worrying, isolating time. Jenna and I tried our best to continue our work and to look ahead to various adventures and projects, never really knowing when our lives would get back to "normal." We spoke to our friends and family and saw them over Zoom, but we hadn't visited with anyone else in person for months.

In some respects, life was sweet and rich. We had each other. We had time to reflect . . . There was time to *breathe*. And yet the "on-hold" aspect of our lives was suffocating. There was no way to know if, when, or how we'd get back to *before*.

The setting made this rough patch a whole lot smoother, I'll say that. I'd always loved the Oregon Coast. It was a special place—even more special now because it offered such a vast landscape amid a time of lockdown. The beaches were flat, wide, bleak—nothing like Southern California, say, where they're crowded with people, bursting with sunshine and action. Our beaches are empty and long, often stretching for seven miles or more, past cliffs and rugged rock formations—and during those dark, dispiriting weeks early on in the pandemic there was often no one else around.

It was late in the day. Pathetically, I hadn't changed out of my pajamas. Another aimless COVID day had just swallowed me. I couldn't seem to shake the funk that had gripped me since the world was put on pause. I pulled a book off the shelf and plunked down on the recliner next to the window, but I was agitated and couldn't focus on the words in front of me. Distracted, I looked up from my book and stared out at the ocean. A storm was brewing. The wind was kicking up. I could see the sand, tornado-like, whipping along the shore.

The swirling sand reminded me of the snow that had spiraled across the Antarctic ice eighteen months earlier, and I was instantly transported. Back then, I was trying to pull a 375-pound sled across a frigid, desolate expanse of 932 miles, from one end of the continent to the other—an unsupported, fully human-powered, solo crossing of the entire landmass of Antarctica, something that had never been accomplished.

I wasn't just racing history, as it turned out. I was locked in a head-to-head battle with Captain Louis Rudd, a British Special Forces soldier and veteran polar explorer, who was making his own solo attempt to achieve this historic world first.

I remembered that it had taken several days for me to adjust to the insane cold of the frozen continent . . . that my goggles had been frozen by snot and tears . . . that I couldn't see a thing, or hear myself think beneath the howling winds. Mostly, I remembered that vulnerable yet exhilarating feeling of being completely alone for two months, in the middle of nowhere.

My mind flashed back to a specific moment on the ice—one that changed everything.

"Maybe you can go for an extra hour tomorrow," Jenna suggested through the static of my SAT phone. "You know, make up some mileage. A little bit every day."

"I already told you," I said. "I can't pull my sled for more than ten hours per day."

In my voice, I knew, Jenna could hear how defeated I was after just five days on the ice. "It's too heavy," I said in despair. "I'm wrecked."

Jenna was trying to administer a dose of encouragement, and to help me problem-solve my way back into the race, after I'd so quickly fallen behind Captain Rudd on Day One—but I was hell-bent on stiff-arming her positivity with my limiting beliefs.

"I can't go any longer!" I shouted angrily into the frozen vastness—*and* into the SAT phone. My anger wasn't directed at Jenna, of course. She was the most supportive partner I could have asked for. She'd been instrumental in the planning of every detail of this expedition—and now, in the reworking of those plans to accommodate this unexpected challenge from this un-expected challenger, my frustration with my own weakness had reached a kind of boiling point. I worried that my quest to be-come the first human to make this crossing was already doomed.

My luck changed the very next day when I somehow caught up to Captain Rudd for the first time. I noticed his red tent in the distance through a whiteout and realized I'd gained more ground on him than I'd previously thought.

There followed a brief, intense exchange with Captain Rudd on the ice later that morning. We both knew the stakes of this race: a couple years earlier an attempt at a similar solo crossing had ended in fatal tragedy.

"Captain Rudd, I don't wish you any ill will out here, but we're both trying to become the first to complete this crossing, and the intention is to be alone. So let this be the last time we speak," I said, trying to project an air of confidence despite my negative inner dialogue.

For the next long while, we were locked in a silent, unac-knowledged battle, as each of us tried to make a statement of strength and superiority. Two men, dragging heavy sleds, shoulder to shoulder across the endless white, matching each other stride for stride as the hours dragged on, like voiceless prizefighters trading blows.

Somewhere in the middle of these tense moments, I reached the ten-hour mark on my day's effort, my usual stopping point. I was completely drained, but I was unwilling to let it show. I glanced over at Captain Rudd and it appeared he had no intention of stopping either, so I pressed on. I dug deeper than ever before, tapping reserves of strength and will I didn't even know I had, determined not to call it quits that day until Captain Rudd packed it in.

In the end, it came down to which one of us blinked first.

After eleven hours, Captain Rudd waved the white flag. I saw him stop to set up his tent, and I breathed a long sigh. However, I wouldn't let myself quit. Captain Rudd's stopping didn't give me permission to stop myself—rather, it lit something in me to keep going. Suddenly, I was determined to push another hour, to establish my first true lead in this nearly thousand-mile race, and in that turning point moment I realized that Captain Rudd's presence on the ice had forced me to rethink my limiting beliefs and change my mindset.

I went from thinking *I can't* to proving *I can* . . . all on the back of this unlikely battle.

The next day, to maintain my lead and perhaps build on it, I logged another twelve hours pulling my heavy load. The day after that, same thing. I told myself if I could do it once, I could surely do it twice, and then again after that, and so on . . . twelve-hour days, every single day for the next forty-eight days.

▲ ▲ ▲

Back in the cabin, in Oregon, that memory lifted me from my hopeless mood. I got to thinking that although the constant twelve-hour days slogging alone across the ice had at first represented the outer limits of my strength and belief in myself, in the end I'd found more bliss, calm, and purpose in those twelve hours each day than I'd ever known before. Trudging across the ice, my mind had never been so clear and my life had never felt so limitless and fulfilling. Was there a way to find that mindset again without traveling back to Antarctica?

I crawled into bed next to Jenna that night, feeling a little lighter, a little less dejected—as if an inner lightbulb were flickering with a new idea, a new focus.

The next morning, I woke up more energized than I'd been in weeks. I jumped out of bed and excitedly announced, "I'm going for a walk. All day! Twelve hours."

Of course, the idea of going for a walk wasn't unusual. It was one of the few activities allowed during COVID lockdown. And so, Jenna and I had logged countless miles up and down that beach together with Jack, but this morning I had the impulse to head out solo.

Jenna could tell I was onto something; she'd seen me like this before. She flashed me an encouraging smile.

"I'm going to try out a new concept I've got percolating," I said. And just like that I bounded out the front door with no specific destination in mind.

It was a gray day, cold for May, with a brisk wind dancing

along the shore break. I was unfazed by the dreary weather, however, and soon lost track of time as the hours ticked by. My thoughts ran free.

At some point, I felt my phone buzz in my pocket. Instinctively I reached for it, and then I pulled my hand back. Hadn't I had enough screen time recently? Doom-scrolling the news, checking in on social media, binge-watching Netflix—daily life had become a seemingly constant stream of FaceTime calls and Zoom meetings.

I don't need my phone for this walk, I thought, and switched it into airplane mode.

Despite my initial excitement, I didn't think this would be easy. When I was out there on the ice in Antarctica, I had no choice but to be with myself in silence. Here on this gray May morning, I was intentionally seeking solitude to contemplate life, again with no distractions.

As I walked, a constant stream of thoughts bubbled up. I certainly was grateful for all the things that seemed to be going right: my relationship, my community, my health. But equally, I was trying to be honest about what left me feeling unfulfilled. And yet it wasn't a hopeless feeling. As I scanned my mind's darker corners, something about the context of the 12-Hour Walk—being unplugged, untethered from the daily chaos—gave me the space and strength to creatively examine my limiting beliefs and reorient my mindset toward living my best life.

As the sun began dropping into the ocean, I picked up the pace to try to make it home before dark.

Jenna met me at the door with a hug. "How was it?" she said enthusiastically.

"It was an eye-opening experience. There's something to this concept. Honestly, I feel better than I have in months. That walk was just what I needed. I think anyone could benefit from a 12-Hour Walk," I said, embracing her.

I smiled as Jack jumped up to greet me, happy for me to be home as well.

▲ ▲ ▲

So that's how I came up with this idea for the 12-Hour Walk, but to be clear up front: this book is not about me, it's about *you*.

You are the hero of this story. I'm simply here to guide you as you take on a one-day journey that will unlock a Possible Mindset and change your life forever.

The Walk might sound simple—and in a lot of ways it *is*—but there's power in simplicity. And, one might say, *magic*. Without a doubt, the directions are simple to follow:

1. **COMMIT**—Pick a day on your calendar to complete the 12-Hour Walk by visiting: **12hourwalk.com/commit**.

2. **RECORD**—Before you set out on your walk, record a short video of yourself to verbalize your intentions. What limiting beliefs do you want to silence? Describe how you hope to feel when you complete the 12-Hour Walk.

3. **UNPLUG**—Turn your phone on airplane mode before starting your 12-Hour Walk. The 12-Hour Walk is designed to be taken alone, with no external inputs—no companions, no

headphones, no podcasts, no music, no email, no texts, no social media—for the entire twelve hours. Keep your phone with you for safety, but use it only to record a quick video or write a note to reflect on later.

4. **WALK**—Begin your 12-Hour Walk. Just like life, you choose the destination. Remain outside for twelve hours, walking in silence. The setting you're walking in doesn't need to be completely silent, but you do. Maintaining *your* silence is the key. Ambient city noise is okay.

5. **REST**—The 12-Hour Walk isn't a race. Take as many breaks as you need. It doesn't matter if you walk one mile or fifty; as long as you keep moving when you can, you're winning.

6. **REFLECT**—Record a video as you finish your 12-Hour Walk. Ask yourself: How do you feel? What did you discover? What limiting beliefs did you overcome? What do you now feel capable of with your Possible Mindset?

Simple right? Well, maybe not so fast. I see you right there through the other side of the pages already trying to talk yourself out of this, wondering why the hell you picked up this book in the first place. I see your limiting beliefs wrapping their tentacles around your mind as you read this.

You're saying to yourself:

"I'm not fit enough to walk for twelve hours."

"I've got kids, and a busy job, I don't have time to take a whole day to myself . . . and even if I did, I sure as hell wouldn't spend it walking alone in silence."

"Silence? Being alone? I'd get sooooo bored . . . and that

long, alone with just my thoughts—that sounds uncomfortable. No, that's not for me."

If you're brutally honest with yourself, you'll find that the doubts, fears, and pushbacks you're assigning to the 12-Hour Walk are actually the very same limiting beliefs that keep holding you back throughout *all* aspects of your life. The limiting beliefs that keep you from becoming the best, most fulfilled version of you.

That's where the rest of this book comes in. Each chapter will break down one of the ten most common limiting beliefs we face, and show how you can conquer your mind to overcome it. We're going to travel together to exciting places at the edges of the world, but also to terrifying places in our minds. And let me tell you, I'm *not* going to sugarcoat anything.

You'll be stronger for it.

Intimidated? Don't be. You aren't alone. I'll be guiding you on this journey every step of the way, so that by the end of these pages, you'll be ready to take on the 12-Hour Walk and adopt a Possible Mindset, letting go of your limiting beliefs, as you step into your best life.

Most self-help and personal development books fall short because they live and die on the page. Very often, they're filled with inspirational quotes and theoretical ideals to consider, but there's never really an opportunity for the reader to *act* on anything.

Simply listening to me and taking my word for it *won't* result in your adopting a Possible Mindset. Lessons like that rarely stick. What *will* make this book's lessons stick will be your own experience completing the 12-Hour Walk. You'll feel these lessons, live them, breathe them, and internalize them. They'll be etched so deeply into you that there'll be no way to ever forget.

I'm asking you to make a very small investment of your time. One day. That's all—a single day. Understand, I'm not asking you to give that day to *me*. It belongs to you.

Invest one day, conquer your mind, and unlock your best life.

The 12-Hour Walk is for *anyone*. It doesn't matter your age, fitness level, or circumstance. After my walk along the Oregon Coast, I wanted to make sure the concept wasn't just an overly ambitious idea, but something that anyone could put into practice—so you might say that I drafted some test subjects.

The results were unanimously positive. From my old college friend who was struggling to find meaning in his nine-to-five job, to my seventy-seven-year-old mother-in-law, who was questioning how best to optimize her golden years, every person I've known to complete the 12-Hour Walk has arrived at the finish line in a much better place than when they started.

If you're *already* living your best life, there's no need to read further. Do me a favor and set this book down and keep doing your thing.

For the rest of us who still need a boost to get unstuck, read on. Your best life awaits.

PART II

LIMITING BELIEFS

LIMITING BELIEF:
"I HATE BEING UNCOMFORTABLE."

Pain is inevitable. Suffering is optional.

—HARUKI MURAKAMI

I gripped the oars with everything I had.

The waves were coming in violent sets—*boom! boom! boom!*—heaving our small boat with a brutal force that lifted us from the surface and cannonballed us back down.

After getting slammed on all sides by forty-foot swells for the past hour, I was completely soaked. As the freezing water slapped me in the face, sending shivers through my body, the salt water burned both my nostrils and the back of my throat, leaving me gasping for air.

As each wave hit, I wondered what it would feel like to drown in these icy waters—and as the wave walloping continued, I wondered if I was drowning already.

We were in a tiny twenty-eight-foot, open-hull rowboat named *Ohana*, only four feet wide and riding just two feet above the water, attempting to cross the world's most dangerous stretch of ocean—in the middle of a savage, unyielding storm.

My entire focus was on my oars, and it felt to me like the ocean's entire focus was on separating me from them. By now my hands had been frozen into a kind of vise grip, locked into a clawlike position, but with each mighty splash of frigid seawater, the ocean seemed to want to swat the oars from my hands and send us spiraling.

What haunted me in this moment—the thought I couldn't shake—was that I'd chosen to be here. *We'd* chosen to be here—all six of us. We'd put our lives on the line to travel to the southernmost tip of South America to attempt to cross the Drake Passage and reach the mainland of Antarctica in an ocean rowboat. We only had our muscles and grit to propel us forward—no motor, no sail. No one had ever completed this roughly seven-hundred-mile ocean crossing in a fully human-powered vessel.

This storm told me why.

We'd been rowing in three-man shifts—ninety minutes on, ninety minutes off. Because the currents were so strong, we had to be moving twenty-four hours a day or risk being blown hundreds of miles off course. That meant twelve hours of rowing each day, *every* day, with twelve hours of intermittent rest carved into ninety-minute chunks—although try "resting" in a miniature hold where you have about as much room to maneuver as a corpse in a closed coffin.

At least, that had been the *plan*, in relative calm. Here, in relative fury, our objective was to keep the boat turned to face the waves: if we got sideswiped by one of these monsters, we were screwed.

The skies had gone black beneath the storm clouds, so we could barely see beyond our oars. The waves were gaining in intensity—as you'd expect in the middle of a raging tempest.

I was on the oars with Cameron Bellamy, a world record-holding waterman from South Africa, and Jamie Douglas-Hamilton, a Scotsman who himself owned several world records in ocean rowing. We had our backs to our destination, which meant we were trusting where we were going and facing where we'd been—a convenient metaphor that emphasized the blind faith we'd placed in each other, and this journey.

Cam barked out instructions as the wave bore down on us: "Right side! Right side!"

I leaned into my next stroke as if our lives depended on it. My arms felt like they belonged to someone else.

"Left side! Left side!"

I tried to match Cam and Jamie as we swung our bodies forward and pulled through the water—the three of us knowing that a single rogue wave could end our journey.

Just then, our captain, Fiann Paul—a world-renowned ocean rower from Iceland who'd originally conceived the idea for this project—popped his head from the stern cabin and shouted, "All hands on deck! We've gotta get out the sea anchor! We can't row into this storm anymore!"

I was seated in the third position, directly in front of the bow cabin, where John Petersen and Andrew Towne, who'd rowed crew at Yale, were clocking their ninety-minute rest interval.

I banged on the tiny door to their cabin from my seated position and screamed, "Sea anchor! We're putting out the sea anchor!"

Andrew shouted back, through the hatch: "Tell us when we're between waves!"

"We don't want to flood the cabin!" John yelled.

With the icy salt water continuously splashing my exposed face I couldn't see much, so I'd been timing the waves on feel. I thought we had about twenty seconds between swells, and as the next wave thundered down on us I called out to them: "Now! Now! Next one's coming! Move, move, move!"

Andrew and John sprang from the cabin onto the tiny deck, and immediately latched the door behind them and secured the safety tethers on their life jackets to the rope that ran along the hull—a half beat before the next wave pummeled the boat and nearly knocked them on their asses.

Andrew was in charge of the sea anchor, so he pulled it from its dry bag and worked frantically, but delicately, to make sure the ropes weren't knotted or tangled.

"Aaagghhh, these gloves!" he screamed after a frustrating few seconds, as he peeled the thin neoprene from his hands with his teeth, hoping his frozen fingers were up to the task.

As he struggled, we kept getting hammered by wave after wave, rocked from side to side, this way and that, as the three of us on the oars tried to keep our boat aligned against the swells.

With an assist from John and Fiann, Andrew was finally able

to deploy the sea anchor—a massive parachute that unfurled beneath the surface of the water and kept us from being blown wildly off course. When it engaged—suddenly, dramatically—it yanked the boat with such force that we were pulled backward, like a pit bull choked at the end of its leash.

After finding our balance, we secured our oars and grabbed on to the waist-high ropes on the side of the fiberglass boat that led to the two small cabins at either end. There we'd ride out what was left of the storm.

As the first mate, I'd been alternating with Captain Fiann, trading shifts in the stern cabin, managing the rudder and navigation. The rest of the crew alternated, two at a time, in the slightly larger hold at the bow, but now that we were at sea anchor we were forced to double up. That meant two men in one hold, and four crammed in another. When I'd been alone in the stern cabin previously, the space was so small that even crouched in a fetal position, my head was just inches from the ceiling. Now trying to escape the storm, Fiann and I hurriedly wedged ourselves into the stern cabin together.

So there I was, sharing these few square feet with a six-foot-one, 190-pound Nordic beast who hadn't bathed in a week. Imagine stuffing two grown-ass men into the trunk of a Honda Civic—you get the picture.

We assumed our positions—our arms and legs wrapped around each other in an awkward spoon.

We were bone-cold, bone-tired, drenched, half-sitting in a couple inches of stinking seawater. If one of us moved, or even twitched, the other one had to adjust to accommodate. Due to seasickness, I'd puked a bunch of times early on in the voyage, so we were bathed in the smell of stale vomit and sea sludge and man sweat. Worse, Fiann was in the habit of eating dried fish that he kept in oil-soaked bags, and it was the most rank-smelling thing ever!

"This is how I'm strong," he'd say, pinching off each bite while I tried not to retch.

We were getting smacked around by a relentless assault of waves, our heads thumping against the walls or the floor or each other.

"How much longer, do you think?" I said during one brief lull.

"Who is to know?" Fiann answered in his clipped English.

After a while, it started to feel like these long, miserable moments would never end, but there was no tapping out. Like I said, we'd all chosen to be here. And yet of all the extreme situations I'd gotten myself into over the course of my adventures— from Everest to the icescape of Antarctica—this was one of the *most* unpleasant . . . one of the *most* difficult to endure.

I was hurting. Bad. All over. The tight, claustrophobic conditions inside the hold pushed me to a place beyond anxiety. It was almost unbearable. Strike that: it *was* unbearable, and yet I had no choice but to bear it. Plus, I was cramping and aching in ways I couldn't address, with no room to move. Everything hurt, from the shooting pains in my fingers to the pins-and-needles burning sensation in my numb toes. It dawned on me that perhaps this voyage had been doomed from the start.

There had been red flags all around.

▲   ▲   ▲

Tempers had been flaring among our crew in the run-up to our voyage. There were mechanical issues with our boat. The rudder wasn't working properly during the test row.

The biggest, clearest sign that maybe we weren't meant to row the Drake Passage was that we were setting out in the middle of a Chilean national tragedy. While making our way to our start point, a Chilean Air Force plane crashed in the middle of the Drake on its way to a military base near Antarctica, killing all thirty-eight people on board—a terrible sadness that hung a black cloud on our departure.

As we were en route from our staging grounds in Punta Arenas, Chile, to launch our rowboat at Cape Horn, we were startled by the blaring sounds of emergency sirens.

"Stand down!" came a disembodied voice, through a bullhorn. "Stand down!"

I looked back and saw a large Chilean Navy ship, which seemed to have emerged in the water out of nowhere. It had pulled up alongside the *Braveheart*—the larger vessel that was carrying our rowboat to the start line.

The bullhorn, again: "We are coming aboard your ship. Make way."

Suddenly, a half-dozen Chilean military officers boarded the *Braveheart*, carrying large guns. It was terrifying, maddening, surreal . . . mostly surreal.

"The Drake Passage is now a military crash site," the leader of this group announced. "You will follow us to our naval port and remain there until further notice."

"Further notice" to Chilean military officials meant "until after we complete our rescue and recovery efforts," which could take weeks, and by then our window to attempt the crossing would be closed.

I looked on from the bridge of the *Braveheart* and tried to make sense of the standoff. On one side we had these intensely serious Chilean Navy officials, dressed in their austere dark uniforms with black berets. On the other side we had the *Braveheart*'s crew of salty Kiwi sea dogs wondering what was going on and why it had anything to do with them. *Braveheart*'s captain went back and forth with the military officials, and for a while it looked like our project was over before it even started. Thankfully, it was negotiated that if we agreed to alter our planned rowing route slightly we'd be allowed to begin our crossing.

Now that I was stuffed into these close, pungent quarters at the stern of the rowboat, getting tossed every which way by an angry sea, I looked back on those dark, tense moments as an omen of the dark, tense moments to come.

I mean, what the hell had we been thinking, rowing our boat through a mass graveyard? How did we not see this plane crash as the mother of all red flags?

▲ ▲ ▲

And yet here we were—and here we'd be in the middle of the Drake Passage battling this storm, for the next long, terrible while.

I ran through a quick self-assessment.

I asked myself, *Am I uncomfortable?* (Yes!)
Am I in pain? (Yes!)
Does this situation completely suck? (Yes!)

My mind raced—from the signs we should have seen, to the signs that were now in front of me.

Another chilling sign: I looked out the small porthole in our cabin door and saw through the fogged glass the blurry image of one of our crewmates. I couldn't see who it was at first, so I wiped the condensation from the small window and leaned in for a closer look. It was Cam, his arms lashed to either side of the boat, his head being whipped from side to side each time a wave battered the deck. From the way he sat, from the way he was being jerked forcefully from side to side, it looked like he was being drawn and quartered in a town square.

He could have been swept overboard at any moment.

As miserable as it was here in the stern hold with Fiann, conditions were apparently far worse for the rest of the crew.

I got on the radio that allowed us to communicate with each other, cabin to cabin. I could only imagine that conditions in their two-man hold in the bow were far worse than what we were enduring in our one-man hold at the stern.

"What's he doing out there?" I inquired. "Cam."

"No room for all four of us inside," I heard back. "We're taking shifts. Four and a half hours in the cabin, ninety minutes one man on the deck. We'll swap out soon."

"Oh, man," I said. "That's fucking brutal."

Then, another voice: "Better one of us out there than four of us in here."

I found myself empathizing strongly with my teammates just across the way. They were in a terrible spot. We all were.

All told, we were on sea anchor for nearly twenty-four hours—a seemingly endless stretch in the most miserable conditions. Toward the end, I was so delirious, so numb, so beaten down by these thunderous waves that I drifted off for a couple beats—or maybe I was knocked momentarily unconscious by the turbulence. When I woke with a start, the storm had finally passed. The boat was still—not entirely still, but still enough. The ripping winds that had filled the air like a primal scream were mostly silent. Fiann must have zoned out, too, because he was coming to the same realization, at about the same time, and as we untangled our limbs and opened the stern hold, we were struck by a rush of brilliant sunlight. We stepped gingerly onto the deck and marveled at the stillness of the water, the blue of the sky.

In the distance, I spotted an albatross soaring above us, and I followed it as it sat itself down on the surface of the water, right next to our boat—another convenient metaphor for the weight we'd just carried and had managed to set aside.

Across the way, our crewmates awakened to the same scene—three of them slithering from the bow cabin and rousing the fourth, who'd been riding out the last of the storm on the deck.

Cam, for one, was oddly in the mood to celebrate.

He stretched to his full height, and from the way he stood it looked like he'd never stood so tall. Like the rest of us, he was feeling on the edge of defeat after the storm—but, unlike the rest of us, he was out to do something to change that.

He held his arms wide, as if embracing the new day, and cried out, "Boys, I'm going for a swim!" Then he stripped off his wet clothes—no easy thing, with the way everything had been soaked through and was now clinging to his skin.

Picture it: this naked man, laid bare in the middle of the Drake Passage, in freezing temperatures. It was the most unexpected, most hilarious, most strangely uplifting thing. The rest of us looked on and shared in his joy, but we weren't about to join him in the water. It was insanely cold!

Cam dove into the ocean with such force the boat rocked with his weight, and as we swayed to compensate, we were in the ocean with him—in spirit, at least. As he swam about fifty feet from the boat in the icy water that ran to a depth greater than ten thousand feet, I was struck by the irony of it all: the very waters that had just blasted us and seemed to want to kill us were now sparking feelings of freedom and joy.

To be clear, we were a long way from done. At this sweet point of pause, we were at about the halfway mark in our voyage. There'd be other storms, other seemingly endless stretches holed up in those awful cabins. When the weather allowed, we resumed our rowing rotations: ninety minutes on, ninety minutes off. When the weather kicked up again, we scurried back into those holds and returned to our shared misery.

▲ ▲ ▲

Finally, after twelve days, with the world's most treacherous ocean miles behind us, we'd nearly reached the end of our journey. The last miles were magical beyond words. The skies were once again clear, the water once again calm.

On one side of the boat, a humpback whale danced across the surface as if to greet us.

On the other side, hundreds of penguins dive-bombed from their perch on a nearby iceberg.

My cheeks burned from the huge smile plastered to my face as I took it all in.

Hands down, it was one of the most glorious, most thrilling sights I'd ever seen. Such abundance! Such breathtaking natural beauty!

We'd done it! We'd become the first people to ever complete this crossing in a fully human-powered rowboat. We battled all of the storms in the ocean and in our minds, and now we were here in this Shangri-la, beaming with pride and camaraderie.

When we could see the shoreline of Antarctica—coincidentally on Christmas Day—Andrew handed me a gift from one of our cabin's holds. A flare.

"Land fucking ho!" he said as he lit the flare.

He lit one for each of us, and we held them aloft in triumph. It was gorgeous, mind-blowing . . . as I knew it would be. As I knew it *had* to be. Because I'd known all along, deep down, that moments of victory can be built only on top of moments of struggle.

HOW THIS STORY APPLIES TO YOU

How do you measure your days?

I measure my days on a scale of 1 to 10, with a 1 being the

worst possible day and a 10 being the best, most euphoric, most spectacular day.

Here's how I look at it: the ebb and flow of our days is like the swing of a pendulum, with the peak arcs representing our 1s and 10s.

You can't have one without the other. That monster twenty-four-hour storm, being tossed by the violent waves like a spec of sand in a sandstorm, was at the bottom of the bottom, the worst of the worst—very much a 1. That day when we finally made land after a nearly two-week nightmare at sea, in the embrace of all those penguins and whales, all of that incomparable natural beauty, was the best of the best—an absolute 10.

And yet that moment as we approached the shores of Antarctica wouldn't have hit me with such transformative force if I hadn't experienced all those prior miserable moments. You could have transported me to the very same spot via a luxury cruise ship and shown me the same sights, but it wouldn't have felt the same. Oh, it might have registered as a 6 or 7, because it was pretty damn great, but what made it a full-on 10 was the struggle and discomfort I endured along the way—all of which was necessary to achieve a goal of this magnitude.

What I've realized is that our 1s and our 10s are connected. To fully experience our highest high, we have to touch our lowest low . . . *and* we have to be willing to push ourselves from what I call the "zone of comfortable complacency," between 4 and 6. The sad truth is, that's where most of us live most of the time.

A deeper truth is that by developing a Possible Mindset we can train our minds to enjoy the 1s—or, at least, to look forward to them. Really. I don't resist those moments of pain and distress, because I know they'll take me to moments of pure ecstasy. A mantra that has helped me—and that I want you to remember—is my version of the quote at this chapter's beginning: *Pain is mandatory, suffering is optional.*

Think back through your own experience and recall your moments of absolute joy and satisfaction and you'll see that your 10s were built on the back of stresses and strains—your 1s. Embrace the 1s. A fulfilled life—*your* fulfilled life—depends on that.

In many ways, our modern society drives us to the zone of comfortable complacency. Most people are stuck in the 4–6 range and miss out on the full experience life has to offer. We're disinclined to take on risk or endure difficulties that might threaten our equilibrium and disrupt the predictability of our days. The American Dream, for example, is all about buying a comfortable house in the suburbs, working nine to five, and being happy with two weeks of vacation.

But is that really your dream? I believe most of us hunger for more—some sort of adventure that will measure what we're *really* capable of.

Too much of life is settling for *good* not *great*, with a lot of time spent in the "eh, can't complain" zone. Let's say you've got a nine-to-five job. You don't love it, you don't hate it. It's something you do to pay the bills. One day, your boss might yell at you for missing a deadline or messing up a presentation, but that day is really just a 4 on your pendulum swing, because you don't care enough about your job for your boss's disappointment to register as a 1.

Let's say you start to do really well at work. You're up for a promotion, or some kind of industry award, but the recognition doesn't really push you beyond a 6—again, because you're not so deeply invested that these honors make a meaningful difference.

One last illustration: you're hanging with your best buds, drinking beers, cheering on your favorite football team on a weekend afternoon. The day might rate a 6 if your team happens to win. If your team loses, it's a 5—because, hey, you were with your bros. Or maybe it's a 4, if you lost money on the game.

We need to push ourselves, challenge ourselves. We need to go from *good* to *great*, to slog through some difficult times to reach pure joy and euphoria.

Discomfort is often the toll that must be paid to achieve fulfillment.

I don't experience my 10s *in spite of* my 1s. I experience them *because* of my 1s . . . and you will too.

Take a moment to think about your relationship to the 1s. Do you go out of your way to avoid them? If you do, you're not alone—most people would rather sidestep the discomfort that comes from taking risks or going to extremes. For some, the risk-reward equation doesn't always add up—meaning, it's not worth enduring sustained hardship simply to taste a moment of victory.

But here's a news flash: the reward that's waiting for you on the other side of this hard stretch *is* worth the price of getting there.

People ask me all the time if I'm afraid of death. They hear about my adventures in a rowboat in the Drake, or on the ice in

Antarctica, or on the frigid peaks of K2 or Everest, and want to know what's going through my mind when I'm up against it, in the teeth of danger.

My answer almost always surprises them.

"Obviously, I don't want to die," I say. "But what I'm really afraid of is *not* living."

We spend our time fearful of experiencing the 1s, but what if instead we chose to fear living in the zone of comfortable complacency every day? What if what we *really* should be afraid of is the baseline condition of "just fine" and "okay" or "good enough"?

I'm sorry, but "good enough" is just not good enough. Not for me. Not for you.

Feeling alive in moments of pain is far more interesting than just existing in the numbness of the middle. It's fine to visit your comfort zone from time to time. In fact, it's necessary—to refresh, recharge, refocus. But let's be clear: Growth happens *outside* the comfort zone; it happens in that insanely cramped stern cabin in the middle of an unrelenting storm. It happens when you risk everything to start your own business. It happens when you step back and watch your daughter cross the street by herself for the very first time.

It happens when you embrace a Possible Mindset by leaving behind the zone of comfortable complacency and entering more dangerous waters, telling yourself that the discomfort you're taking on *can* be navigated and that the 10 you seek does lie up ahead.

KEY TAKEAWAY

Embrace the 1s

Are you living a life of quiet desperation? Are you stuck in the zone of comfortable complacency, stuck between 4 and 6, nimbly trying to avoid feeling any discomfort? Unshackle yourself from that mindset. Seek challenges that take you outside of your comfort zone. In so doing you'll experience some discomfort — perhaps even a few 1s—but trust me, it'll all be worth it when you bask in your next 10.

HOW THIS APPLIES TO YOUR 12-HOUR WALK

Moment of truth: this walk won't be easy. You might be comfortable for the first five or six hours. But there'll be a time when your feet will start to hurt. Your legs might cramp. Endure it. Embrace the pain. Remember, pain is mandatory, suffering is optional. Celebrate the 1s you'll hit in Hour 7, Hour 8, Hour 9 . . . and keep going. Fight through the low moments and let them carry you to the finish. The 10 you'll experience when you return to your front door will inspire you to keep intentionally stepping out of your comfort zone to live your most fulfilled life.

WITH A <u>POSSIBLE MINDSET,</u>

I love stepping out of my comfort zone because it leads to fulfill-ment.

Scan the QR code
or visit **12hourwalk.com/chapter3**
to view a short video that illuminates
the story from this chapter.

4

LIMITING BELIEF:
"I'M NOT A _____."

Life isn't about finding yourself. Life is about creating yourself.

—GEORGE BERNARD SHAW

"**G**oddammit!" I cried out, bracing for impact as my boat started to flip.

I held on the best I could, fighting the inevitable, and when it looked like I was about to capsize I took a deep breath and held it as I went down with the ship.

The boat fell on top of me—a mess of oars and fiberglass overhead. I scrambled to free myself from the foot straps at the vessel's front, so I wouldn't be trapped underneath. I panicked, but only for a brief moment, until I swam out from under the boat . . . and then . . . and then . . . I stood up! One of my feet happened to touch the riverbed and I realized I was standing in just two feet of water.

I was knee-deep in the Willamette River, a couple feet from

the dock where my new rowing coach Chris Wojda was laughing hysterically.

"Yup, you're not a rower," he said, trying to stop laughing. "Let's say we try again?"

Confession: I'd never been in a rowboat before committing to rowing across the Drake Passage. I'd never gone boating at summer camp, never fished from the middle of a mountain lake, never even sat with a girl on one of those "Tunnel of Love" rides at an amusement park. About the closest I'd come was a rowing machine at the gym. No question, the idea of becoming the first to cross the Drake in a rowboat was absurd—and yet here I was.

Yep—me, the guy who'd just face-planted into two feet of water. The guy who couldn't even take a full stroke on this first pass. It was humiliating, dispiriting, frustrating . . . but, hey, it must have been pretty damn funny to a guy like Chris.

Turned out it was also pretty damn funny to this sweet-seeming older woman in a loud sun hat, who just happened to be on the river in her own single scull. She flashed me a mock thumbs-up as she passed. "Pretty rough out here today, huh?" she said with a chuckle.

In truth, the water was calm—not quite like a glassy lake at dawn before the wind can ruffle the surface, but close. So not only was I left wondering what had made me think I could take on this over-the-top Drake Passage journey, but I now had to suffer the indignity of being teased by a stranger.

I didn't consider myself a rower—not just yet—but the thought of putting myself in an extreme environment and fighting my way over, around, or through it held tremendous appeal. So I grabbed at it before I was well and truly ready, which explained how I'd come to embarrass myself in this way under the watchful eye of a guy I'd just recruited to help me out.

▲ ▲ ▲

About that. I'd reached out to Chris just the week before. He was a local rowing coach, and we had some friends in common, so I pegged him as someone who could maybe help get me up to speed. I asked him to lunch, told him I had a project I wanted to discuss. He was already seated when I arrived, at a street-side cafe in Portland, just a few blocks from the first house I lived in as a kid. He stood to greet me.

"Look at you!" I said, as he unfurled his six-foot-eight frame and wrapped me in a bear hug. I'd forgotten how tall he was. "What are they feeding you?"

He laughed—a full-throated, full-bodied laugh that would soon become way too familiar. "Haven't seen you since your solo Antarctica crossing, Colin," he said. "Amazing stuff, man. I followed the whole thing."

"Thanks, Chris," I said. "Means a lot. Believe it or not, I'm headed back to Antarctica again in a few months. That's what I wanted to talk to you about."

We sat back down.

"Antarctica, huh?" he said. "The call of the wild."

"Not just that," I said. "This time, I'm headed there in a rowboat, across the Drake Passage."

Chris shot me a puzzled look—one that seemed to say, *Who the hell is this guy, thinking he can row to Antarctica?*

I filled him in. I told him about the expedition, which was scheduled to begin in three months, relayed how I'd gotten Discovery to produce a feature-length documentary of the crossing called *The Impossible Row*, and described the other rowers I'd be teaming up with on the journey.

"Wow," Chris said, after I'd laid it out for him. "Wish I could say I was jealous, but don't know that I'd be up for a trip like that. Ocean rowing is tough, man. Tell me about the boat. Are you sweep rowing or sculling?"

To Chris, this was a simple question, like asking me if I was left-handed or right-handed.

To me, he might as well have been asking me to split the atom.

"Uh," I said, "what's the difference?"

He looked at me like I'd gone mad. "You can't be serious?" he said. "You're about to do this insane thing in just three months."

"That's actually why I called you," I said. "I'm not a rower . . . yet. I need help."

Chris patiently explained how sweep rowing was when the oarsman has both hands on a single oar—like you see in collegiate rowing in an eight-man boat. In sculling, the oarsman holds one oar in each hand and is responsible for powering both sides of the boat.

"That one," I said sheepishly, without a whole lot of confidence in my answer. "I think it's that one."

Again, Chris looked at me like I had a couple screws loose,

and for an awkward moment he didn't say anything—he just kind of stared at me. I think he knew what I was about to ask of him, and he was trying to figure me out.

I moved to fill the silence. I said, "Three months isn't the problem. I'm supposed to meet the rest of the crew in Scotland in three weeks for a test row to begin training as a unit. The Discovery production team will be there, and I don't want to make a fool of myself."

"Three weeks?" he asked, with a puzzled look. "That's not a lot of time."

"Tell me about it," I said.

Next, Chris reasonably asked if I'd been doing anything at all to train for this trip, so I told him I was back working out with my dear friend and coach Mike McCastle.

"You remember my strength coach, Mike?" I asked.

Chris nodded. I knew that if he'd been following my solo trek across the frozen continent, he was probably aware of the crazy Mr. Miyagi–type workouts Mike had come up with to prepare me for the extreme polar conditions I'd face on the ice—but just to be sure I pulled out my phone and queued up a video from my Instagram feed.

Most of the people who followed me on social media knew Mike McCastle was like a brother to me. He was relentless—not just as a trainer but as a card-carrying badass in his own right. He'd held the world record for most pull-ups in twenty-four hours—5,804, smashing the mark of 4,030 set by another well-known badass, the ultramarathoner and retired Navy SEAL David Goggins. Mike had pulled a 2.6-ton Ford F-150 for twenty-two miles across Death Valley, one of the hottest places on Earth, flipped a 250-pound truck tire the distance of a half-marathon, and climbed a rope the vertical equivalent of Mount Everest in just over twenty-four hours.

Some of his training methods were diabolical, but they were inspired, and effective as hell. I trusted him with my life . . . and athletic career.

"Here," I said, handing Chris the phone. "Check this out."

In the video, Mike was having me do planks with my hands in ice buckets, and then a series of squats with my feet in ice while solving a bunch of Lego problems with my frozen fingers to keep my mind and dexterity sharp.

"Might seem strange," I explained to Chris, narrating as he watched, "but these simulations Mike created in the gym literally saved my life when I was alone in Antarctica. We couldn't go to Antarctica to train, so Mike brought Antarctica here."

"That's great. Mike is incredible, love him," Chris said as he handed back my phone, "but what about the Drake? Those waters are nasty and cold and treacherous. No way he can simulate *that* here in Portland."

"Don't be so sure," I said. "Mike is nuttier than ever with this one. Just the other day, he pulled me out of bed at two a.m. Jenna was in on it, she'd given him a key, and there he was, shaking me awake, standing over me in the dark. I thought I was having a bad dream, but he shouted at me to get my ass out of bed and get to work."

I told Chris how I was still half-asleep, half-out-of-my-mind when Mike dragged me outside and put me through another one of his wild workouts—this one designed to simulate a frantic, furious (and freezing!) ocean crossing. He'd set up four Bosu balls, onto which he'd balanced a standard rowing machine, so the apparatus was rocking and swaying in ways I could expect in those turbulent waters. As I rowed, he kept dousing me with buckets of ice water at irregular intervals, the water burning my face and slapping me awake; the whole time he was peppering me with basic math and current events questions to make sure I was dialed-in mentally as well as physically.

In his own way, Mike was testing my commitment, my courage, my clarity of vision to confront the challenges I'd face in some of the most threatening waters on Earth.

Chris didn't seem convinced that a series of inventive workouts could get me where I needed to be for this expedition—or turn me into a rower. It wasn't an add-water-and-stir type of deal. He was right to be skeptical: I was totally *not* a rower, although I felt confident about meeting this challenge.

Chris must have sensed my determination as I talked animatedly about the project over lunch, however, because he agreed to work with me. The more we chatted, the more his demeanor seemed to soften. What came across, I think, was that I'm most comfortable outside my comfort zone. That's where I live and breathe. I'm drawn not only to doing things that have never been done before, but to doing things *I've* never done before.

"I know what you're capable of, Colin," Chris finally said, "so this isn't bat-shit crazy. But I've been rowing for more than

59

twenty-five years, and I still have a lot to learn. I'd be worried if it was me planning to do this row. But I can maybe teach you a few things, lay some foundation."

I jumped up from the table in excitement. Really, I was so completely pumped he was willing to help me, so grateful.

Chris said that in the short time we had we could work on my posture, my timing, and my muscle memory. He thought that if I could flash-train my body to work the oars to precision, I'd at least be able to fall into rhythm with the other rowers and find a way to power through.

"Meet me at the dock Monday morning," he said. "Five a.m. sharp. We'll see what you've got and start there."

▲ ▲ ▲

So that explains how I came to be standing in knee-deep water on this quiet stretch of the Willamette River, red-faced, just a couple feet from the dock, while Chris looked on, his giant frame doubled up in laughter as I pounded the surface in frustration.

I felt like a fraud—the poster boy for imposter syndrome. I wasn't used to broadcasting my inexperience in such a public way, but here I was, with no good reason to think I had a chance of pulling this off.

One thing it would have helped to know was that these sleek one-man sculls were wobbly as hell. You had to kind of strap your feet into the rowing station while somehow keeping the boat in balance—only, as I'd just learned the hard way, if you let go of one of the oars to reach for your feet, say, the vessel would roll with you.

"You've got to feather the blades!" Chris hollered at me from the dock, motioning me to turn the oar blades parallel to the water for stability, as I struggled to get back in the boat and self-correct. "Rowing 101. Never let go of the oars."

And so, I feathered the oars, just like he'd demonstrated.

I reached for the foot straps and wrapped my feet back in the Velcro ties—one hand on the oars, one hand working the straps.

The boat shook and tottered as I leaned forward and tried to maintain my balance, thinking, *This shit is way harder than it looks.*

I took a deep breath and prepared to take off, hoping not to embarrass myself a second time in these nothing waters.

"Okay," Chris hollered. "When the boat is stable, square the blades and take a stroke."

Blades in . . . arms engaged . . . legs pushing.

I took my first stroke, and then a second. By the third stroke, the dock had started to recede into the distance, and when I saw that I'd gone about fifty feet, I let out a triumphant cry.

"*I am* a rower!" I screamed. "*I am* a rower!"

Of course, I was no such thing, but I was on my way.

HOW THIS STORY APPLIES TO YOU

When you look in the mirror, do you see yourself only as you are? Or do you also see the person you'll become?

Being able to see the person I'd become was how I was able to make the leap from never having rowed a boat to rowing the Drake Passage.

How I got there was by changing from a fixed mindset to a growth mindset—concepts originated by Stanford psychology professor Carol Dweck. I went from thinking in terms of what I *can't* do to what I *can* do.

A fixed mindset says, "I'm this person in this moment, and I'll never be anything different." You tell yourself you're good at math but not very creative—or that you have an ear for music but not for languages. It's what it is, and you are who you are . . . end of discussion. These fixed notions become a part of your identity, in such a way that you're not very likely to grow or change or try something new.

A growth mindset says, "I may be this one person in this moment, but there's no reason I can't grow, evolve, and learn to be any other type of person in the next moment." It's the idea that through hard work and determination, you can learn and improve.

Embracing a growth mindset is a crucial component of living with a Possible Mindset.

Say you went to law school and have been working at a large firm for the past twenty years. Recently, you were struck by a great business idea. But then your fixed mindset kicked in. *I'm not an entrepreneur. I'm a lawyer. I bill hours, that's what I do.* Do me a favor. Fight that urge. Sure, you aren't an entrepreneur just yet, but there's no reason you can't become one. Allow your growth mindset to own this new identity, and just start the process.

We all have to start somewhere, right?

Think about it: every single person who has made an impact in their field started from a place of inexperience. Kobe Bryant would have never changed the landscape of basketball if he hadn't stepped on the court one day as a kid and taken his first shot. Janis Joplin wasn't a generation-defining musician until she picked up a guitar and played her first chords. Meryl Streep wasn't an actress until she auditioned for her first school play. Stephen King had to sit down and write the first sentence of his first book before he could write his sixty-fourth novel. These game-changing artists and athletes didn't wait until they were at the top of their fields to own that part of their identity. They simply woke up one day and began the process.

Today can be that day for you. This. Very. Day. Say it out loud:

I am a basketball player!

I am a musician!

I am an actress!

I am a writer!

I am a rower!

Whatever fixed image of yourself you're carrying, set it aside. Claim your new identity. Write it down here.

I am a _____.

(*Really*, grab a pen and write it down. Go ahead. I'll wait.)

Make it a part of your life. Hell, put it in your social media profile, if that's what it takes to get your head around the idea. Whatever it is you want to be or do or try, give it voice. Work toward it. Own it. Internalize it. Change your mindset and achieve anything. Know that whatever it is you *don't* know how to do, you can *learn* how to do. (Hey, that's what Google is for, right?)

Also, know that you might stumble a time or two as you

find your way, just like I did when I flipped over on that shallow stretch of the river. That's part of the deal. Prepare for it. And tell yourself *before* you face-plant into the river that when you do, you'll pick yourself right back up and get right back at it. Know that these initial struggles are the keys to growth and learning . . . they're *not* failures. The only failure is in not trying.

One of the fears that keeps many of us from stepping out of our lanes is that we might feel like we don't belong, or that the people around us are stronger, smarter, or better. *Imposter syndrome* is a real thing. I know I've felt it on many occasions—not just that morning on the Willamette River.

You've probably experienced it on the first day of a new job, or maybe at a dinner party with a bunch of people you don't really know who seem to be way more successful—that sense that you don't quite fit in or that you're somehow not worthy. But try to remember that everybody at your new job probably had the same first-day jitters. Those way more "successful" folks seated around the dinner table—they've all felt overwhelmed or overmatched at one time, until finding their way. The key to their success isn't some big secret, it's actually quite simple: all of those people eating and animatedly swapping stories woke up one day and had the confidence to believe they could grow and evolve into the people they've become. You're *not* an imposter, you do belong.

So go ahead, look in the mirror and see the person you hope to be, claim your identity. *Become* the person you hope to be. Today.

KEY TAKEAWAY

You are a rower (or whatever you want to be)
Stop telling yourself that you aren't this or you can't do that. That's just your fixed mindset talking. The key to unlocking your fullest potential is to embrace a growth mindset. You can be anything, you can do anything. Stop looking in the mirror and being disappointed with who you are right now, and start seeing in your reflection the limitless possibilities of who you can become.

HOW THIS APPLIES TO YOUR 12-HOUR WALK

Likely, you've never walked twelve hours in one day. This will be new. At the current moment you aren't a "12-Hour Walk finisher." By adopting a growth mindset, you'll realize you're capable of finishing this new challenge. Once you've completed the 12-Hour Walk, you'll have proven to yourself that having a growth mindset in all elements of your life will allow you to *be* and *become* anything you set your mind to.

WITH A <u>POSSIBLE MINDSET,</u>

I can learn, grow, and become anything.

Scan the QR code
or visit **12hourwalk.com/chapter4**
to view a short video that illuminates
the story from this chapter.

5

LIMITING BELIEF:
"I'M BROKEN AND
WILL NEVER BE THE SAME."

Emancipate yourselves from mental slavery, none
but ourselves can free our minds.

—BOB MARLEY

"**M**ake it stop!" I screamed. "Please, make it fucking stop!"

I'd never imagined such pain was possible—the kind of pain you'd expect in a torture chamber, on a battlefield, or in a chainsaw massacre . . . not in a hospital.

The lower half of my body had been completely burned, and it felt to me like my legs were still on fire, like I was being stabbed by hot knives, like there were bugs crawling all over my skin. I'd suffered such severe second- and third-degree burns that my nerve endings were all exposed—and now that my pain meds had been discontinued, I was in absolute agony.

I wasn't sure I believed in God, but here He was—in my prayers, in my pitiful cries for help, all around.

"Please God, make it stop! Fucking hell!"

My mother had flown halfway around the world to be at my side and love me through these unbearable moments, but even she couldn't fill the spaces where the pain meds had been.

"Colin," she said, her chair pulled close to me in my hospital bed. "I don't know what to do. Tell me how I can help you."

Her demeanor was calm, but I could see she was trying to keep it together for me. Inside, I knew, she was terrified, heartbroken, but she didn't want to let it show.

"Make it stop," I cried. "Get them to give me something to make it stop." I was sobbing, screaming, squirming in agony. There was no end to it.

I was lying on my back in a Thai hospital, in a coarse paper hospital gown, my legs thickly bandaged from my toes to my waist, but not so thickly bandaged that I couldn't see the blood and puss seeping through the gauze and the tape. It was a horror show. I couldn't look . . . I couldn't *not* look. My legs were in a half leg lift, suspended in midair—the only way to get even the smallest bit of relief from my own deadweight pressing down on those open nerves.

I'd just been transferred from a bare-bones local hospital on the island of Koh Samui, in the Gulf of Thailand, where the paint on the walls was chipped and peeling, where a feral-looking cat danced across my bed in what passed for the ICU, where a doctor came to examine me four days into my ordeal and announced in broken English that I'd never walk normally again.

Earlier that day, as I was being loaded into a medical transport plane, a nurse had come and yanked the fentanyl drip from my arm. I was too out of it to question her. My mom was doing her best to manage my transition to Bangkok's bigger hospital and spoke up.

"Hey," she shouted, protective of my care, "he needs those meds!"

"The medication," the nurse said, "it's for here." And with that she walked back to her vehicle on the tarmac of the small island's airport.

My mom locked eyes with me as she sat beside my stretcher in the back of the cramped plane. We were both confused and overwhelmed by all that was happening.

The one-hour flight to Bangkok by air ambulance was all my ravaged body could handle. I couldn't stay in that hospital on Koh Samui, but I couldn't go far. There was no way I could travel all the way home to the USA in my fragile state, so it was agreed that I'd fight this battle in Thailand. Unfortunately, by the time we arrived at the more modern hospital in Bangkok, I was reeling, my pain meds now fully worn off. The nurse doing my intake explained that she couldn't just shoot me up with a full dose of intense opioids, and besides it was the middle of the night and the pharmacist wouldn't return until 8 a.m.

"Too much medicine," she said, trying her best to communicate with me in English. "Too much, one time. Too much, dangerous. You have wait till morning."

My mother sat by the bed in my new hospital room and tried to distract me from the pain. She was sunny, and hopeful, although I realized later that she didn't want me to see how completely freaked out she really was. In the moment, it must have been anguishing for her to see her child suffer in this way, but she tried to lift my spirits in whatever ways she could.

As a happy distraction, she started telling me for the millionth time about the song that she had played on repeat when she gave birth to me at home on a hippy commune twenty-two years earlier—Bob Marley's "Redemption Song."

"That song got me through," she said.

It was the last song Bob Marley recorded before he died, and the first song I heard as I came into the world.

I'd always loved this story, but just now I didn't have the patience for it. There was no distracting me from the throbbing, stinging, burning sensation in my legs—that is, until my mother started singing this heart-lifting, heart-healing song of freedom that was as much a part of me as air. The singing was something to distract us, she told me later, a place to put her energy, her emotion.

After a couple verses, I joined in, at the top of my lungs:

"Redemption Songs! These songs of freedom!"

For me, it was a place to put my pain—a way to step from the hell I was in and into a more peaceful state.

Over and over, we sang that song—louder and louder each time out. The door to my room was open, because my mother had thought it might light a fire in the staff if they could hear my screams, but now that we'd started channeling Bob Marley, I couldn't guess what these people were thinking. We were singing, screaming at the tops of our lungs—for almost eight hours! Despite myself, despite my torment, I'd lapsed into an almost trancelike state, a meditation . . . until finally, mercifully, I collapsed into a deep sleep.

▲ ▲ ▲

Eight days earlier, I'd been on a beach in the Gulf of Thailand with my best friend David Boyer. It was early 2008 and we were on what was meant to be the postcollege trip of a lifetime—and it was, it turned out, but not in the ways we'd imagined. We were out and about one night when we noticed a flaming jump rope exhibition down the beach from where we were staying.

Stupidly, I joined in, and in a split second my life changed. I got tangled in the fire rope and was immediately engulfed in flames. In a panic, I wrestled free of the fiery rope, which had been doused in kerosene, and instinctively ran into the ocean to extinguish the flames, where I felt a flash of relief. Stepping out of the surf, I looked down at my body to see large swaths of skin hanging off me like charred wallpaper in a condemned house.

Somehow, David got me to a makeshift clinic—down a dirt path on a moped! After I was transferred to the more modern hospital in Bangkok, I stayed on for over a month, until the doctors said it was safe for me to travel. In all that time, my mother stayed by my side—nursing me, loving me, coaxing me through this horrendous ordeal. It was superhuman, really, the way she hung in there with me.

Each day, my mother sat with me and advocated for me and

tried to lift my spirits. One day she turned to me and said, "Colin, let's set a goal." Her sunniness and positivity were still shining through.

I pushed back, asking, "What goal? I just want my life back."

She said, "Come on, a *real* goal. A tangible goal. The doctor says you'll never walk again normally. Tell me how you'll beat the odds. Do me a favor, close your eyes and visualize something positive."

I finally took her suggestion seriously, and I closed my eyes and gave it some thought. For the first time in a long time, I smiled.

She saw my expression change and said, "What? What do you see?"

I closed my eyes, and somewhere in the fever of my mind I could picture a body of water, a bike, a long and winding road. I said, "I see myself crossing the finish line of a triathlon."

To her great and everlasting credit, my mother didn't laugh or tell me to visualize a more *realistic* dream. She just hugged me and smiled and said she'd help to make that happen.

Persuaded by my mom to come up with a goal, I had tried to picture my best self, and so I thought back to when I was a kid, watching the Kona Ironman Triathlon on television for the first time. I hadn't realized it was a deep-seated desire of mine to cross a triathlon finish line, but here it was. All it took was putting the aspiration out there and giving it voice to make it seem possible.

▲ ▲ ▲

72

A month or so later, I was finally released from that Bangkok hospital and cleared to fly home. I was carried on and off a series of airplanes and pushed around in a wheelchair. My legs were heavily bandaged. I still hadn't taken a single step.

The day after I returned to Portland, I sat with my mother in the kitchen, in the house in which I'd grown up, not yet realizing that this would be the day the rest of my life would start. Every day, my mother and I had talked about my goal of completing a triathlon. We'd held the prospect out in front of us like a carrot—or more accurately, a lifeline. But on this day, my mother pushed me to action. She sat across from me and said, "Today, your goal is to take your first step."

She pulled a wooden chair from our kitchen table and set it out in front of me in my wheelchair and said, "Today, you're gonna get out of that chair and step over to this one."

I looked down at the wrap on my legs and saw the blood and scabs through the gauze and tape. I knew my legs had begun to atrophy beneath those wrappings—shit, they were no bigger than my arms! The muscle mass I'd spent a lifetime building had vanished. The fresh skin coming in at my knee and ankle joints was so tight that I had little to no mobility, so I knew it would take every bit of fight I could summon to take that one step.

I sat in my wheelchair for three hours before mustering the courage to take my first step and stood on my blistered and bandaged feet before collapsing again into the wooden chair.

But my mom didn't let me quit. She kept pushing me. The next day she moved the chair five steps away, the next day ten.

It was an arduous progression, but a progression, nonetheless. With each step I was willing myself whole. Trouble was, I was still living in my mother's basement, still hearing those ominous words from the Thai doctor who'd essentially told me my life was over.

You will never walk normally again.

So far, he was right—and despite my being able to hobble around for brief periods, I was feeling depressed and left behind. It had been almost two years since I'd graduated from college. Everyone I'd gone to school with was out there in the world, making noise, working, living on their own, and I knew I needed to get on with my life.

▲ ▲ ▲

I started applying for jobs. My uncle Neal helped me land my first real interview, at a commodities trading firm in Chicago. The company flew me in to meet with the owner. I remember stepping gingerly into the elevator of their downtown office building and pressing the button for one of the upper floors—the 44th, I think. I was alone. I caught a glimpse of myself in the elevator mirror. I was dressed to impress: a crisp, white-collared shirt; a tie my mother helped me pick out; a perfectly pressed pair of pants. I gave myself a once-over, from head to toe, making sure I was good and ready. Shirt: check. Pants: check. Confidence: check.

But then as my eyes dropped, I saw I was wearing a pair of fluffy bedroom slippers. My heart sank . . . and my confidence fell right along with it. I thought, *Oh, yeah those.* My feet were still messed up. I'd been burned to a crisp, couldn't wear shoes.

74

That explained the slippers, which had become such a fact of my new life that I'd come to accept them. They were a part of me. Trouble was, in the safety of my own home, I never had to think how they looked. Out here in the real world, they didn't exactly set the right tone.

I couldn't be sure, but it felt to me like the receptionist was looking at me funny when I stepped off the elevator. You know that feeling, when you realize you've got a piece of food stuck in your teeth and wonder how many people you've interacted with since you last ate? You're mortified, but you're not quite sure *how* mortified? I was already self-conscious about walking with a limp and an uncertain gait, and now it was sinking in that I'd dressed for a big-time job interview as if I were going to a slumber party.

I approached the receptionist and gave my name. She told me someone would be out to see me shortly and directed me to a seat in the waiting area.

"Anything I can get you?" she asked as I stepped away from her desk. "Water? Coffee? A cold beverage?" *A pair of shoes?* I imagined her asking next.

In retrospect, I realized she was simply extending an office kindness—a standard show of hospitality she'd have offered any visitor. At the time, however, it felt to me as if she viewed me as fragile—that my slippers signaled I was weak or off or less than. And as those anxious minutes in the reception area ticked by, I went from believing I was ready to ace this interview to thinking I wasn't ready at all.

I tried to play it cool. Of course, when the CEO stepped out to greet me, he noticed my feet straightaway. He was a big, tall guy, with a swagger I'd come to associate with many of the movers and shakers in the building. He cracked a small smile—a look more of bemusement than amusement.

A voice inside my head said, *So much for dressing to impress, Colin.*

He indicated my feet with a subtle nod and said, "Slippers?"

I was humiliated, that this was the first impression I'd made, but I tried to shrug it off. I'd come this far, I thought. I wasn't about to let a pair of fuzzy bedroom slippers keep me from beginning the rest of my life.

"It's a long story," I said.

▲ ▲ ▲

I shared the long story in the interview, and a few other things besides—and I ended up getting the job. And when I moved to Chicago a short time later, I fell into a routine. Each day, I managed to walk a little farther, in a little less pain. I was nowhere near where I wanted to be, but I would shed my slippers soon enough and do a passable job of seeming "normal."

By the time I started work, I'd graduated from slippers to proper dress shoes.

One day, when most of my colleagues had already clocked out, I reached under my desk for a bag containing sneakers. I was spotted by John, whose desk was next to mine. We were around the same age, but he'd been at the firm longer. He'd started his career the moment he graduated college. We both officially reported to senior management, but he was my de facto boss. As he put on his coat and scarf, he saw me stepping out of my dress shoes and into my new running shoes.

He caught my eye and said, "It's pretty nasty out there today. Bundle up."

"You bet," I said, quickly moving to leave the office.

"What's with the sneakers, Colin?" he asked.

"I'm training for a triathlon," I said, like it was the most natural thing in the world.

"Wait, what?" he shot back. "I see you every day, and you can barely walk."

I smiled, looking down at my running shoes. "Actually, to jump-start my training, I've committed to walking to and from work."

"So you're about to walk home?" John asked, incredulous.

"Every day," I said proudly.

John knew where I lived—about a half-hour walk from downtown. "Are you out of your mind?" he asked. "It's seven degrees Fahrenheit out there. The wind is whipping off the lake. Nobody walks around Chicago in the middle of winter."

"Nobody but me," I said, lacing up my shoes. And with that, I bounded off into the Windy City evening, ready to take on the world . . . one step at a time.

▲ ▲ ▲

The kicker to this story is that summer I made it to the start line of the Chicago Triathlon. I got there by degrees, and by design. After banking all those miles walking back and forth to work, I joined a gym not too far from my office. I swam in the pool. I rode the stationary bike. Eventually, I started running on the treadmill. I was deathly afraid of falling on the streets of Chicago in winter and scraping up my legs before they had a chance to heal, so I did most of my training inside. Each day I did a little bit more . . . until I was finally able to step to the start line on the day of the race and dive into Lake Michigan and swim my first mile.

I didn't just complete the race as I'd hoped, but by some sweet mixture of grit and willpower I *won*, placing first overall in a field of over four thousand. But the real victory for me was just being there, eighteen months after closing my eyes and visualizing myself in that moment.

I'd set the race out in front of me like a pipe dream and found a way to make that dream come true.

HOW THIS STORY APPLIES TO YOU

No matter how you've been broken, you have the power to build yourself back up. If you're weak, you can make yourself strong. If you're shattered, you can put yourself back together. If you're wounded, know that you can heal.

I wouldn't be where I am today if my mother hadn't taught me to set a goal for myself in that Bangkok hospital room. A lesson that would become a core tenet of the Possible Mindset.

I wouldn't have taken on any of the *out there* or *impossible* projects that have defined my life since winning that triathlon.

I wouldn't be writing this book . . . that's for damn sure.

But that's the thing about goals. Realistic, seemingly unrealistic—it doesn't matter. When you visualize what you want to accomplish, when you give it voice and agency, you begin focusing on all of the positive possibilities. And when you're broken in the way I was broken, when you've been told that your life will never again be the same, you can either accept your fate or fight like hell to retrieve what you've lost—maybe even get to a better place.

On the scale of 1 to 10 I wrote about earlier, my burn accident was a 1. It hurt. It sucked. It caused a ton of people a ton of pain . . . not just me. But there's no denying that it opened a door to all these 10s that followed. It forced me to focus on what I wanted out of life, and the hard work necessary to *get* there.

So go ahead and open the door to the 10s that are waiting to be discovered. If right now you're struggling to believe in yourself, know this: *I* believe in you.

Let's take the first step toward *your* chair together. Just like I did in that Thai hospital picturing myself crossing a triathlon finish line, if you feel broken, I want you to close your eyes and visualize yourself whole. What do you see? What are you doing? How does it feel? Hold on to that vision and keep it sharp in your mind.

Now that you've defined your big goal, your Everest, you'll see how simply having it can speed you down the road to recovery. You know I love big goals, but in this exercise big goals can be a trap since they often feel so far out of reach that we don't know where to begin.

This is where the next step comes into play. The most important step.

Ask yourself: *What single incremental step can I take today to get me one step closer to that big goal? What small step forward is within reach?* No step is too small.

What is *your* "wheelchair to the wooden chair" moment? Take that step, and then push the chair farther away tomorrow. Commit to taking at least one incremental step forward each day, and you'll be amazed at how quickly you'll be swapping your slippers for sneakers, ready to cross your "triathlon finish line" before you know it.

No question, there are injuries, disabilities, and illnesses that deny us the chance to ever be the same—and there's no piece of hard-won advice or motivational strategy I can share to turn back that kind of circumstance. And yet I'm constantly inspired by stories of people overcoming giant obstacles and moving themselves forward. The man who was paralyzed in an accident but went on to become a prolific artist using his mouth to paint. The woman who was born without legs, but still went on to win sixteen gold medals at the Paralympic Games. The lifelong skier who blew out her knees and took up whitewater kayaking as a new way to push herself. They all show us the power of the human spirit; each reminds us that our potential to thrive is limitless with the right mindset.

If you've ever broken a bone or faced a daunting procedure like a knee replacement surgery, you've probably heard an orthopedist say that when the bone heals it'll be stronger than ever, or alternatively, that the man-made parts in your new knee will be more durable than the God-given parts ever were.

The same applies to whatever it is you're facing: You'll be

stronger tomorrow than you are today. You'll be more capable tomorrow than you are today. Maybe not in the same ways you were once strong and capable, but in all the ways that matter.

The story of my burn injury is a lesson in the power of incremental goal setting, but it's also a lesson in perseverance and grit and positive thinking—all of which are crucial components of a Possible Mindset. I'm no different from you. If I can take steps, so can you. We all have the capacity to shift our mindset toward the positive and imagine a brighter future.

Go ahead and reach. Push forward. Build yourself back.

KEY TAKEAWAY

Swap your slippers for sneakers
You might be injured. You might be dealing with a setback and wondering if you'll ever be the same. Or you might be frustrated that at a previous time in your life you were stronger. This situation doesn't have to be permanent. Remember, I set all my world records *after* I was broken. You, too, have the power to rebuild yourself. Set an incremental goal. Take your first steps. Swap out your slippers for sneakers.

HOW THIS APPLIES TO YOUR 12-HOUR WALK

Understand, the 12-Hour Walk isn't *just* an exercise in physical endurance. It's not even *mostly* an exercise in physical endurance. There's no prize for going farther or faster. The 12-Hour Walk is *all* about training your mind. If you can only make it around the block once because your knee is barking, fine. Slow down, take a long break. Injuring yourself isn't the goal. You can still log your twelve hours by sitting alone with your thoughts, with no outside distractions. The mental strength you'll gain from this challenge will move you at least one step closer to overcoming your current physical setbacks.

WITH A <u>POSSIBLE MINDSET,</u>

I can heal, even if I've been broken. I can stand back up, even if I've been knocked down.

Scan the QR code
or visit **12hourwalk.com/chapter5**
to view a short video that illuminates
the story from this chapter.

6

LIMITING BELIEF:
"I'M AFRAID OF
WHAT PEOPLE WILL SAY."

Criticism is something we can avoid easily by saying
nothing, doing nothing, and being nothing.

—ARISTOTLE

"I think I'm going to quit my job," I said into my phone.
Silence.

"Grandma Sue, are you there?"

"Yes, I'm here," she said. "I'm just trying to think of a more
subtle way to say this, but I'm coming up blank, so here it is.
That's a terrible idea, Colin."

Then more silence.

I'm not sure what I'd been expecting. Grandma Sue had
been generally supportive of my life decisions. She was a proud,
hardworking Chicago native, and had raised my mom and her
four siblings there. Just that morning she had been the only

member of my family at the finish line of the Chicago Triathlon, and she'd taken me to breakfast after the race to celebrate my surprise victory. And yet her response just now left nothing to interpretation.

I'd just finished telling my grandma how, after she dropped me off at my apartment following the race that morning, my friend Jenny Gelber had invited me over to her parents' house for a barbeque. Over the course of the evening I got to talking with her father, Brian Gelber, a legendary commodities trader. I told him about my burn accident eighteen months earlier, my childhood dream of competing in the Olympics, and the triathlon win that day. He'd offered to sponsor me if I wanted to reignite my dream and chase a triathlon gold medal at the Olympics.

I'd made it clear to my grandmother that he wasn't offering me a pile of money, just enough to buy a few plane tickets to races and spend my days training. I'd underscored that this "offer" was nothing like getting drafted by an NBA or NFL team. If I accepted, my lifestyle would be taking a major step back financially.

"Colin, it was amazing to witness what you did out there today, but that was just for fun. You're an adult now, my dear. You need to be realistic," Grandma Sue said, with a heartfelt yet admonishing tone.

"But I've always dreamed of being a professional athlete, and maybe this is my last shot," I pleaded, trying to convince myself as much as her.

"Look, as your grandmother I've always tried to encourage you to follow your own path, but it's also my job sometimes to knock some sense into you. Remember what happened last time you passed on a secure future and went backpacking around the world instead?" She didn't need to fill in the blank—we all knew the pain, and disruption to the family, my burn injury had caused.

She continued, "Besides, what would you tell Uncle Neal? He pulled some serious strings to get you that job interview. Take *him* as a role model; he's raising four great kids here in Chicago, and a career in finance has given him a great life. Don't you want the same? Now's not the time to throw it all away."

"Yeah . . . I hadn't thought yet about what I'd say to Uncle Neal . . . ," I said, feeling my previous excitement deflate.

"After all of the hard work and sacrifice you put into earning your economics degree, it's time to stop playing around and put your education to use. You have a bright future ahead of you," she said, leaning into what I'd be giving up with my recklessness.

Grandma Sue was a hard person to argue with.

"Okay, thanks for talking it over with me," I said, ending the call shortly after.

My triathlon gear was strewn on the floor near the door. I tossed my phone on the coffee table and walked over to pick up my soiled race clothes and flung them into the stacked washer and dryer set nestled in the closet. It was the first time I'd lived on my own where I didn't have to walk to the basement with a handful of quarters to do my laundry. It occurred to me that my new, ready-to-use appliances might be a perk that would go away if I cast aside my first "real" job to chase dreams of athletic glory.

I wasn't ready yet to drop the idea of racing triathlon full-time, so I picked up my phone again and called my friend Eric. As a peer, surely he'd have a better perspective on this than my grandma. We'd been close in college, and after each of us landed jobs in Chicago, we'd been nearly inseparable, grabbing happy hour after work, staying out late on weekends, watching sports— the typical big-city, young professional life.

"What's up, man?" I said, then jumped right into it with no small talk. "I'm thinking about quitting my job."

"What? Did you get a better offer at another trading firm or something?"

I walked him through how my day had gone—the triathlon win, the sponsorship offer, and my uncertainty about what to do.

"So what do you think?" I asked, finishing my explanation.

"Where would you live? How would it all work?"

"Well, this is all new, so I haven't totally figured it out. But I met a professional triathlete and former Olympian named Simon Thompson this weekend, and he told me that most guys train in Australia in the winter months, you know 'cause it's their summer so the weather is ideal for training. Simon told me he'd introduce me to his coach in a place called Canberra if I wanted."

"So you're going to quit your job? And move to Australia? Where are you going to live? Like you'll rent an apartment there?"

"I won't be able to have a full-time job and also train for the Olympics, so I'll probably have to move into a shared house or find a couch to sleep on for a while. I did that kind of thing when I was traveling before Thailand—it wasn't so bad."

"Dude! I just googled Canberra. Have you looked this place up?" I could hear him laughing while he clicked his keyboard. "It's the capital of Australia, but it's not even on the coast. I'm reading a travel forum called '10 Reasons Why Nobody Should Travel to Canberra.' This place looks awful."

I was pacing around my apartment at this point.

"I haven't looked it up yet, man. Like I said, it was just one idea." He could tell I was getting frustrated with his tone.

"Do me a favor, Colin. Look outside your window. What do you see?"

"Downtown, uh, the Sears Tower . . ."

"That's right, the Sears fucking Tower! Big city, big future," he continued fervently. "You've got a sick apartment, an amazing job, and we've been crushing it at the bars lately. What more do you want? Don't quit your job, man. There's so much for us here. It's only just the beginning. Sounds to me like a classic case of the Sunday Scaries. Get some rest. You'll feel better tomorrow."

"You're probably right. Thanks for the pep talk. See you to-morrow for happy hour."

"G'night, and congrats again on the triathlon, amazing stuff. Would be cool if you won it again next summer."

I slumped down on my couch. My body was exhausted from the long and intense day, but my mind was still racing. I turned on the TV and flicked through the channels hoping something would capture my attention. But after about fifteen minutes of channel surfing, I tossed the remote, grabbed my keys, and walked out the door.

I needed to clear my head, and I thought, maybe, an evening stroll would help.

▲ ▲ ▲

I aimlessly wandered through the city streets. I could smell the summer breeze coming off the lake and hear the familiar sound of the L train skittering down the tracks overhead. Questions pinged through my mind: *What's the right path for me? Could I really leave my job and chase my Olympic dream instead? What'll everyone say if I do?*

Well, I already knew what my grandmother—and probably, by extension, my uncle and my friend Eric—would say. *They'll tell me I'm a complete fool!*

Sometime later, I returned to the lobby of my building and took a right turn down the hallway past the elevator bay to check my mailbox before calling it a night. I put my key in the lock and found nothing but junk mail inside.

An older gentleman, probably in his fifties, with salt-and-pepper hair, walked into the mailroom just then. I recognized him from the building. He was always stylishly dressed. We weren't friends, but I'd exchanged small talk with him in the elevator a few times, and noticed he lived on the top floor.

"Michael, right?" I asked.

He smiled back and said, "Yeah, good to see you. How was your weekend?"

Typically, with a relative stranger I'd normally respond with something simple like "Fine" or "Pretty good" and move on. We all know that when it comes to exchanging pleasantries, the person asking isn't usually looking for the *real* answer. But in my confused state I couldn't help myself, so I unloaded a somewhat truncated version of my weekend on Michael.

And finished up with "So, I think I might quit my job and move to Australia. What do you think?"

"First off, congrats on the triathlon, that's a helluva story," he exclaimed, nodding, seemingly impressed.

He locked his box, and holding his small stack of mail, he tossed his keys in his hand and posed an unexpected question back: "Have you seen my car? The Porsche Cayenne?"

"Yeah, the black one. I've seen you leave the garage, it's nice."

"Look, we've all felt the call of adventure from time to time. I can see how in your mind quitting your job, and moving abroad, looks appealing right now, but the point is, I didn't get to where I am, a great career, a comfortable life, by making rash decisions. My advice, since you're asking, would be to stick with your job, your career path. Trust me, when you're my age, you'll thank yourself for not throwing it all away on a whim."

He gave me a small pat on the shoulder and walked out of my existential crisis as quickly as he'd entered it.

▲ ▲ ▲

I awoke the following morning to the familiar sound of my alarm, perfectly timed so I could execute my standard morning routine: brush my teeth, shave, shower, get dressed, and walk the thirty minutes to work.

I ducked into the break room and grabbed my morning coffee, before heading to my desk on the firm's trading floor. Like usual, I arrived there thirty minutes before the market opened. It was an open floor plan. I had ten screens stacked on my desk displaying charts, graphs, and multiple markets; they remained open at all times so I could analyze and execute trades.

This was my time each morning to get up to speed on the overnight movements in the Asian and European markets before the bell rang in New York. But as I opened the news feed on my Bloomberg terminal, I couldn't focus.

I called over to my boss, John, who was seated at the desk to my right. "You got a minute to chat in the conference room?" I inquired.

"Sure, what's up?"

As we walked into the conference room, which consisted of a dozen high-backed leather chairs and minimalist decor surrounding an oversized center table, John twirled a pen in his hand and closed the glass door behind me.

"Congratulations on the triathlon by the way. A few guys from the office texted me about it last night. I can't believe you won. Unreal. You've come a long way since you were wearing those slippers," he said, chuckling.

"Thanks, it's been quite a whirlwind." I hesitated, trying to choose my next words carefully. "About that. After the win, I got offered a sponsorship, and I wanted to talk to you about putting in my two weeks' notice." The blood left his face.

As the words left my mouth, a part of me tried to hedge or backtrack.

"I mean, I haven't fully made up my mind yet, but I'm sort of considering it," I said, wavering.

John looked back at me, confused.

"You know," he said, "it's almost the start of Q4, and right after the New Year it's bonus time. Quitting to race triathlon seems like an absurd idea to me, but what *really* doesn't make sense is quitting right now. You might be the only person, ever, to leave your full bonus behind this late in the year. Friend to friend, if you do nothing else at least wait a few months, until after we receive our bonuses."

I'd weighed this aspect over the past twelve hours, but I also knew that if I didn't take the leap now, there was no telling what my headspace would be in a few months, or if the sponsorship offer would still stand.

"The Olympics. I've always dreamed of making the Olympics," I said, trying to find a rational argument for what my gut was telling me to do.

"If all went perfectly to plan, what year would you make the Olympics?" John asked. I could see the annoyance in his eyes now.

"Well, the next Olympics are three years from now in London, but, more realistically, my best shot would be the 2016 games in Rio."

"And how old will you be then?"

"I'm twenty-four now, so I'll be thirty-one in 2016."

"Look," John said, "it's not my life, but we're in the business here of assessing risk and placing bets. The odds of you making the Olympics in a new sport that you just tried for the first time must be infinitesimally small. Assuming you quit today, and then eventually don't make it to the Olympics, what then?"

"Um, I guess I'd try and secure a job in finance again," I said sheepishly, realizing I hadn't thought out that far.

"But you'll be thirty-one, and no firm is looking for an entry-level trader who's thirty-one. You saw how hard it was to get a job in this industry after you took that gap year after college. We took a chance on you, Colin. The door will be shut after this."

He wasn't trying to be overtly mean, or harsh. Rather, he was just stating, calmly, what he believed to be the facts.

"Colin, the market opens in ten minutes, and I need to get back to my desk. Why don't you take that time to think about all of this, and let me know your decision before the bell."

He stood up and left the room.

I sat there facing a large wall clock, watching the second hand *tick tick tick* as my mind played out the scenarios and tried to make sense of all the "advice" I'd received since yesterday.

With three minutes left before the market opened, I'd made up my mind. I walked back out to the trading floor and over to John's desk. *Here goes nothing.*

"I'd like to put in my two weeks' notice. I'm sorry. I just feel that, if I don't take this opportunity, I'll always wonder what could have been."

John looked up from his chair, his hand on his chin, and nodded slowly. "So that's your final decision? Your final, final decision? You sure?"

I paused. "Yeah, I'm sure. I'll wrap up anything here that you need over the next couple weeks and—"

He interrupted me, moving his hand from his chin and opening his palm to face me like a traffic cop's. "Okay, stay right here, don't touch anything, I'll call security."

The blood left *my* face now. I looked back confused.

"Colin, there's no two weeks' notice in this industry. When

you're done, you're done. There's too much proprietary information at stake. It's nothing personal, it's just standard protocol."

As I tried to form a sentence, a security guard I recognized from the lobby bounded toward us in long strides. He was neatly dressed in a suit and tie and had one of those Secret Service–style earpieces in his left ear. It was as if, in the seconds after my "final decision," I'd gone from being a trusted friend and colleague to a criminal suspect. The security guard looked at me with cold matter-of-fact eyes.

"Grab your personal effects and let's go. Don't touch your keyboard, your computer, or any papers on your desk, sir."

In a rather out-of-body moment, I stepped over to my workstation and grabbed my gym bag from underneath my desk. Repeatedly, I glanced at the security guard, moving deliberately like when you're pulled over for speeding by the police and cautiously reach into the glove box for the registration paperwork. I took a quick scan and realized there was nothing else that belonged to me.

"I guess that's it," I said, looking over at John and hoping for more than I would get.

"HR will follow up through your personal email about any last paperwork and your final paycheck. Good luck," he said, shaking my hand. And then the security guard ushered me out of the office and into the elevator.

It was a silent ride down to the lobby, and as the elevator doors opened the security guard turned to me.

"Key fob?"

Man, these guys don't mess around. I pulled my work badge out of my pocket and handed it over.

I walked through the revolving door and onto the street. As the chill of the morning air hit my cheeks, I looked back up at the glass tower above, disoriented by the rapid sequence of events. *There's no turning back now*, I thought, conscious that there'd be many more critics as I followed my heart and stepped into my new life.

HOW THIS STORY APPLIES TO YOU

How many of your heroes *weren't* criticized along the way?

Spoiler alert: it's a trick question.

Anyone who's ever achieved great things has been criticized by someone, at some point. When you decide to break free from the zone of comfortable complacency to unlock your best life, be sure to strap on your armor because the critics are coming.

Have you ever had an experience like the following? You post to social media about something you're excited about—say, you're announcing to your community that you're going to train to run your first marathon. Several people leave kind and uplifting comments, like:

"Yay, congrats."

"You're going to crush it (bicep curl emoji)."

At the end of the day you're scrolling down your post and see that someone has left a negative comment, "Why would you do that? Seems like a waste of time!"

That night you struggle to fall asleep as you replay the negative comment in your head. You act out in your mind what you'll say to that person the next time you see them—to put them in their place. And in the worst case, you start to *believe* the critic. You ask yourself, *Is running a waste of time? Should I not be training for the marathon?*

Our prehistoric brains are hardwired to be negatively triggered by criticism. That's because, when we lived in caves, the feeling of shame or not belonging was a warning sign that we wouldn't survive if the tribe abandoned us. Despite this dependency on the group no longer being as extreme in modern life, our DNA still triggers the fight-or-flight response as a defense mechanism to criticism.

The worst thing you can do is to try to avoid criticism at all costs while never "daring greatly" to live out your full potential.

To me, Teddy Roosevelt summed this up best when he said:

> It is not the critic who counts; not the man who points out how the strong man stumbles, or where the doer of deeds could have done them better. The credit belongs to the man who is actually in the arena, whose face is marred by dust and sweat and blood; who strives valiantly; who errs, who comes short again and again . . . who at the best knows in the end the triumph of high achievement, and who at the worst, if he fails, at least fails while daring greatly, so that his place shall never be with those cold and timid souls who neither know victory nor defeat.

Don't let one social media comment stop you from pursuing your goals. Don't let the fear of what others might say stop you from chasing your dreams, no matter how silly or unrealistic they may seem to others. This is *your* life, and with a Possible Mindset you have the power to decide exactly how you want to live it.

I thought telling my grandma that I quit my job was hard. Years later, I found out what hard *really* was when I started telling people that I planned to walk across Antarctica alone. Imagine how many versions of "that's a terrible idea," "don't do that," "it's impossible," and "you're going to fail" I heard when I announced that expedition.

Countless. But that didn't stop me from trying.

When I returned home from my successful solo crossing of Antarctica to global acclaim, I quieted the critics who originally told me it was a bad idea. However, an entirely new group of critics raised their hands, saying disparaging things like Colin's crossing was "achievable" and "contrived."

You'll rarely, if ever, be criticized by someone who's living their best life. Chances are, those people will know—and respect— the challenges of your pursuit. More often, criticism comes from those who're disappointed by the outcomes of their own lives and need a target for their frustration and insecurity.

Is there a time and place to listen to constructive criticism, advice, or feedback? Yes, absolutely. The key is learning how to discern constructive criticism from destructive criticism.

Take into account the source.

If you're being criticized by a stranger on the internet, that one is easy: ignore it; this person doesn't actually know you.

If you're being criticized by a family member, colleague, or close friend, take a breath and hear them out. My grandma, for example, was genuinely trying to give me her best advice, based on what *she* thought my best life should look like. Often, people close to you can offer valuable feedback and a helpful perspective. They can even, like a mirror, reflect back to you what you've said you want, and realign you if you're not living your truth. However, be careful not to *blindly* follow their lead. In my case, in deciding to quit my job, I trusted my intuition (we'll go deeper on intuition soon). Remember, you know *you* better than anyone else. There are times when you need to override the well-intentioned criticism of family and friends.

Regardless of what you do, people are going to talk—they'll have an opinion about it. You can't control what others are going to say, only how *you* react.

In fact, here I am, giving you my best and well-intentioned advice on how to unlock your best life. It's up to you to decide if my advice is worth taking.

Keep in mind: you won't look back at the end of your life and say, "I'm really glad I avoided criticism." If you always bend to the opinions of others, you'll look back like that gentle old man by the elevator in the penthouse in Manhattan, wondering what would have been possible if you'd dared to live your truth.

It's not too late. Don't let *anyone's* criticism stop you from entering the arena.

KEY TAKEAWAY

Step into the arena
When criticism inevitably comes your way, take a moment to consider its source, and be discerning about whom you choose to listen to. Step up to the plate, take the shot, strive valiantly, dare greatly in all that you do, and disregard the "cold and timid souls who neither know victory nor defeat."

HOW THIS APPLIES TO YOUR 12-HOUR WALK

Welcome to the perfect opportunity to test the strength of your new armor. Likely, when you tell people about your commitment to completing the 12-Hour Walk, some will instantly respond with criticism, saying things like "That's a horrible idea, why would you do that?" Trust that your Walk will lead to monumental breakthroughs. You might even find that once you're living your best life, those who initially criticized you will find themselves inspired by your transformation and choose to dare greatly themselves, attempting their own 12-Hour Walk.

WITH A <u>POSSIBLE MINDSET,</u>

I can dare greatly, even when facing potential criticism.

Scan the QR code
or visit **12hourwalk.com/chapter6**
to view a short video that illuminates
the story from this chapter.

7

LIMITING BELIEF:
"I'M AFRAID OF FAILING."

I've missed more than 9,000 shots in my career. I've lost almost 300 games. 26 times, I've been trusted to take the game-winning shot and missed. I've failed over and over and over again in my life. And that is why I succeed.

—MICHAEL JORDAN

*I*t's important a Brit cracks this journey first.

Those words echoed in my head as I stared at one of the most intimidating men on the planet, British Special Forces Captain Louis Rudd.

The smell of stale jet fuel and rust penetrated my nostrils. We were crammed with hundreds of pounds of our individual survival gear into the back of a tiny Twin Otter plane, bound for the outer edge of the Antarctic landmass where we were about to begin a two-month, head-to-head race across the frozen continent.

It wasn't just the plane that was shaking—my confidence was

also less than sturdy as we approached our landing on the white abyss.

There'd been a long lineage of proud British polar explorers who'd attempted various Antarctic expeditions over the last hundred years or so. Before leaving home, Captain Rudd had told a reporter from the *Telegraph*, "It's important a Brit cracks this journey first." He seemed to think it his birthright to be the Brit who grabbed the glory of becoming the first person to cross the entire landmass of Antarctica solo, unsupported by resupplies, and fully human powered.

Admittedly, he *was* significantly more experienced than I, having completed a couple of historic polar feats already—and shit, he was essentially the British equivalent of a Navy SEAL. But before making this journey to the bottom of the world, I'd proudly told the *New York Times* how *I* planned to conquer this seemingly "impossible first." Now, staring out at the ice through the window of the plane, and then back at Captain Rudd's grizzled face, I wasn't so sure.

As the plane door cracked open at my starting location, the minus-twenty-five-degree air slammed into me like a frozen semi-truck. I quickly snatched up my goggles and face mask before my skin became flash frozen.

The pilots helped me unload my sled and gear onto the ice. My load weighed 375 pounds, full of everything I'd need to survive. I'd be pulling it behind me every day for the next two months.

"Good luck," they said, climbing back into the cockpit to usher Captain Rudd to his starting point.

I'd take all the luck I could get. We'd be racing nearly one thousand miles to reach the other side of the continent. We'd made a gentlemen's agreement to start one mile away from each other, but equidistant to the first GPS waypoint on the route. The tension was high enough already; better we each had a bit of our own space to get started.

The pilots didn't even bother to take off again. Rather, I watched the plane taxi over the uneven terrain, and in a few short minutes the aircraft deposited Captain Rudd on the ice before taking off and leaving us both out there to fend for ourselves.

Antarctica is expansive beyond words. As a sailor experiences crossing an endless ocean, you can see white for miles and miles. With clear skies that day, and twenty-four hours of daylight in Antarctica that time of year, Captain Rudd's one-mile buffer didn't seem like much. I could almost make out his confident expression. I tried to ignore him while packing up my gear to begin, but I could feel his presence with every heartbeat.

My fingers were stinging from the cold as I nestled the final pieces of gear into my sled and strapped into my harness for the first time.

I switched on my GoPro to mark the occasion. "So here and now on November 3, 2018, at 3:22 p.m., I officially begin. Beginnings are simple. You take a step forward. If you're going a thousand miles or a hundred yards, it's the same," I said into the camera with a nervous smile.

My body was revved up like a thoroughbred's, ready to explode from the starting gate. I heaved forward to begin and then . . . nothing. I was stuck in place.

I shook out my legs and arms like a track star getting ready for a race, and tried again. A few steps this time, and then slam, stopped dead in my tracks, unable to move.

I grunted and groaned. Although I could get my sled going for a few steps and at one point a few minutes, I couldn't sustain the effort for long.

I'd known the sled would be at its heaviest on the first day—and by simple math would slowly get lighter from burning fuel to melt ice into water and from eating food, which primarily consisted of custom-designed, whole-food, plant-based nutrition bars called "Colin Bars"—but I'd never imagined that I wouldn't be able to move my sled at all.

The hopelessness began to overtake me like a storm tide washing over the beach.

We all know misery loves company, so I glanced over at Captain Rudd, expecting to find him in the same predicament. I couldn't have been more wrong. What I saw instead was a military man in full march, making steady progress, seemingly without any of my same struggles.

As I watched him disappear over the horizon, I stood in a dazed stupor. My eyes melted into a river of tears, filling my goggles. But what happens when it's minus-twenty-five degrees outside and you start crying? The tears freeze to your face.

"I'm a pathetic failure!" I yelled out to the expanse of Antarctica, falling to my knees.

This wasn't my first high-stakes race. My mind flashed back to a day more than one hundred degrees warmer and a world away.

▲ ▲ ▲

I dove off the pontoon into the crystal-clear, blue Caribbean waters of Cozumel, Mexico. Usually you can see for hundreds of feet in these tranquil waters that are world-renowned for snorkeling and scuba diving. But not today. Instead, all I could see was churned up whitewater. I was like a wet sock being tumbled in a washing machine.

I was battling sixty-five of the top professional triathletes in the world during the first leg of the Cozumel World Cup, the latest stop on the International Triathlon circuit. We were all there vying for world-ranking points, hoping to eventually qualify for the Olympics.

It had been four years since I'd quit my finance job, I was in my fourth season racing as a pro, and I was honored to be representing the USA on the world stage. Yet, after all these years, I still hadn't had the breakout performance I needed to really prove I deserved one of the coveted Olympic spots.

Maybe today was that day.

I'd become friends with many of the guys as we raced and traveled around the world for months at a time following the professional circuit. Yet once the start gun went off and we dove into the water, there was no room for friendship.

We rounded the first turn buoy, and I choked on mouthfuls of foaming seawater. Gasping for air, I fought to stay near the front of the pack, my arms turning like turbines to propel me forward. Open-water swimming is nothing like the civilized pool swimming I was accustomed to as a collegiate swimmer, where everyone had their own lane, and their own space. This was a lot more like a WWE wrestling match.

Despite the battle in the ocean, I tried to remain calm while exiting the water. At which point began one of the most critical parts of any triathlon race—transition.

I ran up the beach, efficiently ditching my goggles, clipping on my helmet, and mounting my bike in a matter of seconds, all while sprinting barefoot.

As I leaped onto my bike and strapped into my bike shoes, which were already clipped to the pedals, I could hear my heart pounding out of my chest. The humid, tropical air filled my lungs and the ninety-degree heat dried the salt water from my skin instantly.

My legs feverishly pumped the pedals as the Mexican fans lining the street cheered us on.

"*Andale! Andale!*" they shouted.

I looked up over my handlebars, taking stock of my position in the race for the first time. Hell, yes! I was in a great position. The words "ESP Gomez" were printed on the red race jersey directly in front of me.

Javier Gomez of Spain—the reigning World Champion and the London Olympic silver medalist, the rock star of our sport—was just a few feet ahead.

I'd never been this close to the best at this stage of a World Cup. It felt amazing! I allowed myself a satisfied smile, feeling for the first time in my professional career that I belonged beside the best of the best.

I wasn't about to blow this opportunity. I stayed glued to Gomez's wheel, allowing his slipstream to carry me forward to the front of the race as the miles ticked by. And then, Gomez surged in the final half mile, solidifying his position in the lead before the transition to the run. And I went with him, matching him pedal for pedal.

I jumped off my bike and as my bare feet hit the pavement, I was neck and neck with the World Champ, heading into the final leg of the race.

We racked our bikes in the transition zone and quickly jammed our feet into our running shoes, adorned with elastic laces that made wasting time tying them unnecessary.

Every second counted.

Stride for stride, shoulder to shoulder, we ran down the palm tree–lined street. *This is it, Colin,* I told myself. *Hang on. Dig deep. You belong, you can beat him, you will make the Olympics, you've got this.*

Until I didn't.

Gomez looked over his right shoulder at me, as he switched into another gear. A gear I didn't have, a gear apparently only reserved for the actual best, not a wannabe like me. And just like that, he was gone.

Stick with it, Colin, second place is still a proud finish in a race like this. I clung to hope. The sweat cascaded down my forehead and burned the corners of my eyes. I tried every positive self-talk trick I knew. I begged my legs to forget their pain and keep pushing.

I cracked, and then I broke.

Another athlete passed me, and then another, and another. I felt like I was going backward. My hopes and dreams were crashing down. The strength and pride I'd felt moments before evaporated, replaced with the nauseous feeling of failure. I didn't belong with the best; I wasn't even second best or third best.

As I dragged myself across the finish line, my stride looking more like that of a wounded dog than a gazelle, I was in forty-eighth place.

I found Jenna in the finish line area as the winner, Gomez, and the other two podium finishers celebrated their success by dousing themselves with bottles of champagne.

"I'm never going to make the Olympics, Jenna. I suck. I'm sorry you had to witness that today," I stated frankly, trying to hold back an all-out meltdown.

Jenna wrapped me in her arms, not caring that I was soaking her clean clothes in sweat and spit. She leaned on her signature optimism, telling me, "Don't be so hard on yourself, Colin. It's one race. And for two-thirds of it, you looked amazing. You've got another shot next week in Puerto Rico. Let's get you cleaned up."

I wasn't feeling so optimistic, but I feigned a smile as we headed back to our hotel.

▲ ▲ ▲

Bang! The start gun went off as we dove into the ocean outside Old San Juan, for the next race on the International Triathlon circuit.

I'd tried my best to wash off the stink of failure from my performance the week before and to wipe the slate clean for this race.

I exited the water, heart pounding again after the inevitable wrestling match in the sea, and sprinted toward my bike. The bumpy cobblestone street sent vibrations through every inch of my body. I was in the middle of the bike pack with about five other athletes.

"Let's go! Let's work together," a Guatemalan athlete shouted to our group, glancing quickly at me. "We can catch the front guys if we all work together."

It's customary in a pro bike race, whether the Tour de France or a professional draft legal triathlon, to work together in a scenario like this. If each guy takes a hard pull at the front, and blocks the wind for the rest of the guys behind him, the collective effort is significantly faster than going it alone.

The five of us quickly fell in line. Each one of us sprinted at the front for fifteen seconds or so, before falling back to the end of the line, and letting the next guy take his turn. We rode just inches off each other's wheels to maximize the draft, mimicking the controlled chaos of race car drivers barreling down the track at the Indy 500.

"We've fucking got this, guys!" I shouted after taking a turn at the front, a burst of energy surging through my legs.

The pace quickened. We all stood up out of our bike saddles, putting maximum power through our pedals as we accelerated out of a hairpin turn. I was just behind the wheel of a Swiss athlete, the current leader of our group, getting ready to take my turn at the front. He peeled off to my left, and as I felt the extra strain of the wind hit my body, I swerved.

"Shiiiiitttttt!" I yelled.

I was suddenly airborne, ejected from my bike, like Superman without the cape.

I hadn't seen the deep pothole in front of me soon enough, and now I was flying through the air, in what felt like slow motion, trying to brace myself for the inevitable. While falling I locked eyes with a spectator who had the Puerto Rican flag painted on her cheeks. She raised her hands to cover her face and gasped in horror at what she was witnessing.

Like a baseball player sliding headfirst into home plate, my body scraped across the rough road. Other than my helmet, I was practically naked. No gloves, no socks, just a paper-thin race suit and bare skin.

For a second everything was silent, I was totally numb, and then in a rush, the searing pain shot through my body.

"*Ambulancia! Ambulancia!*" I heard someone scream.

I rolled onto my back and brought my hands in front of my face to survey the damage, wincing in pain. There was no skin on the palms of my hands, just blood and grime and gravel. My race suit was shredded. It was as if I'd gone headfirst through a meat grinder. The sight of so much skin hanging from my body sent a PTSD shudder through my soul, bringing me back to that Thai hospital years before.

In a merciful moment of shock, I blacked out.

Coming to, I found that I'd been transported back to the

finish line area and placed inside a makeshift medical tent. I was lying on my back atop a table in a pool of my own blood.

"Oh my God. Colin, are you okay?" I heard a voice shout over the din of the crowd still cheering on the other racers.

I would have recognized that voice anywhere. Jenna had found me.

She ran into the medical tent, her kind, loving eyes meeting mine.

I could tell she was doing her best to be strong, but her look of fright told me that I was far from okay.

"Tell them they can't, it hurts too much," I whimpered, feeling the sharp sting of my scrapes.

"Don't worry, Colin. Be strong for me. The doctor just needs to clean out the wounds. It's going to be . . ." Her voice trailed off and her face drained of color.

Jenna's knees buckled. Her limp body careened toward the ground. Thankfully, one of the nurses saw this happening and instinctively cradled her head, moments before she hit the cement. The medical staff abandoned their scrubbing of my wounds, and all reached down to lift Jenna onto the empty table beside me.

It was the blood. Jenna had always been squeamish around blood.

She opened her eyes confused. I could tell by the look on her face that she hadn't quite figured out why *she* was lying on a table with her feet in the air surrounded by medical personnel.

"Here, drink this," the doctor said softly, handing her a cup of Gatorade.

And then we both burst into laughter. If there was ever a

more pathetic duo, I'd never seen it. We couldn't help but belly laugh at the absurdity of the situation. Truth was, though, that my laughter was more a feeble attempt at hiding my broken feelings.

Failure with a capital *F*.

We made our way back to our hotel room a few blocks away, Jenna carrying my scraped-up bike frame and me hobbling, wrapped in blood-soaked gauze, but trying to find the silver lining. At least I hadn't broken any bones.

I turned to Jenna. "I don't think I'm going to make the Olympics," I said, completely raw from the moment.

"Chin up. You got unlucky today," she said, smiling.

"It's not just today. Or even the last four years of professional triathlon, sacrificing everything for this goal. Do you realize I've been working toward making the Olympics for over twenty years? Ever since I watched swimming at the 1992 Barcelona Olympics on TV as a kid. When I quit my job in Chicago, everyone warned me this would happen. Now here I am, just as they all predicted. I've tried. When am I going to admit to myself that I've failed?"

I paused the rant to catch my breath.

"You know, the swim team used to come to Puerto Rico every winter in college for our training trip. Being here again brings back memories. Did I ever tell you about my last collegiate swim race?"

"I'm not sure. What happened?"

I told her the story of that day back in 2006 at the Ivy League Championships when I'd competed in my final 100-yard breast-stroke race, the culmination of fifteen years of competitive swimming. Sure, I'd won numerous Oregon State Championships as well as regional titles, and I'd been ranked as high as fifth in the country for my age in the breaststroke. Heck, I'd been recruited to swim at a Division I university. But those were all incremental steps toward achieving my actual goal, representing the USA in swimming at the Olympic Games.

I shared with her how I'd come off the final turn, ready to leave it all in the pool that day.

Pull. Breathe. Kick. Pull. Breathe. Kick.

With one final stroke I flexed my fingertips and touched the wall. I stared up at the large digital scoreboard to see how I'd done.

"I didn't win. I didn't break any records. I didn't qualify for the NCAA National Championships. I simply didn't go fast enough to qualify for the Olympic trials. Just like that it was over. Swimming, the goal, my dreams. Done . . ." I trailed off.

I remember looking back up at the scoreboard one last time to make sure I hadn't misread the results. My vision blurred. My goggles were filling up, not with chlorine-scented pool water, but with salty tears . . .

▲ ▲ ▲

My consciousness suddenly snapped me back to my predicament on the Antarctic ice. I was again experiencing goggles full of salty tears, this time frozen, and even through the blur, I could tell Captain Rudd was long gone.

I reached for my SAT phone to call Jenna, not knowing what else to do.

"Is everything okay? Didn't you just start? Where are you?" Jenna sounded alarmed through the static of the satellite connection.

"I can't pull my sled. It's just too heavy." I tried to keep my voice steady, but I was certain Jenna could hear it crack amid another flood of tears that I couldn't hold back.

I went on, "I always knew it was possible I'd fail out here. I thought maybe after thirty or forty days alone on the ice I'd be forced to give up for some reason or other. But I'm still basically at the start line, and I already feel like the world's biggest failure. I took all those interviews and announced my goals to the world, and I'm standing here stuck on Day One. Captain Rudd is long gone; I don't know what to do."

Jenna paused for a second. I heard her take a deep breath, and then she said, "You aren't a failure. You're out there in Antarctica. Do you know how many people never even take the first step toward their dreams? Remember what we always say . . . the only failure is in not trying. Forget about Captain Rudd, forget about the race, forget about the media. This moment is for you."

She went on to suggest that if I could just make it to the first waypoint a half mile away I'd feel like I'd made some progress. She encouraged me to set up my tent and get a good night's sleep.

"Tomorrow we'll regroup, and you'll take a few steps more. You'll go a few miles more," she concluded.

And that's what I did. Each day for the next two months, alone on the ice. I battled, I fought, I kept putting one foot in front of the other, trying to find my way until my perceived failure on Day One turned into my brightest success on Day Fifty-Four. After eventually passing Captain Rudd and pulling my sled 932 miles, I became the first person in history to complete a fully human-powered, unsupported solo crossing of the landmass of Antarctica.

HOW THIS STORY APPLIES TO YOU

Failure is a fact of life.

Let me guess, you've failed a time or two. Thank goodness. It means you tried something.

If you're like me, you probably don't remember learning to walk, but I can guarantee you this—you fell down thousands of times as a toddler before mastering the craft. Imagine where you'd be today if after falling down for the first time your one-year-old self had stopped trying and gave up forever.

From the womb we intuitively know that there's really no such thing as failure—that momentary failures are just a series of lessons and learnings that lead to success. But all too often, as we get older, our brains forget this important fact, and we begin to fear failure so acutely that we stop trying to learn and grow.

I failed to make the Olympics.

I tried as a swimmer and then again as a triathlete. I sacrificed my career in finance—much to the disappointment of my family and friends—to chase my Olympic dream. And still, I failed.

And yet I write this book having set ten world records.

I never would've been able to successfully walk across Antarctica alone if it hadn't been for the two decades I'd spent building my physical strength in unknowing preparation for that expedition. I never would've been able to survive the terrors of the

Drake Passage row without sharpening my mind all those years in the pool.

I've succeeded because I've failed.

I learned from my failures, and chose to keep moving forward, to keep trying, to keep aiming higher.

The only thing stopping you from cultivating your own success is your limiting belief. The one that keeps telling you: *Don't start that business, don't ask out your crush, don't share your art with the world, don't apply for that new job.* Your fear of failure is preventing you from setting that big goal and pursuing it.

It's time to abandon that fear, and instead embrace the many benefits of the process.

Let's take entrepreneurship as an example.

Say you risk it all to start a business and for whatever reason it fails and you have to shut it down. Don't get me wrong: that moment will likely be painful, but was it a complete waste of time? Should you have never tried in the first place? I'm guessing you actually had some incremental wins and learned some valuable lessons that can be applied to a future business goal.

I certainly had incremental successes along my path despite my overall failure. Pursuing swimming allowed me to study and get a world-class education even if I didn't end up making the Olympics. Becoming a professional triathlete gave me the opportunity to travel to over fifty countries on six continents. Seeing the world in that depth provided an unforgettable foundation for my relationship with Jenna, even though I again failed to make the Olympics.

I may not have gotten the medal, but I got the girl.

Back to your hypothetical failed business venture. Despite the temporary pain of closing up shop, you surely learned and grew along the way. Perhaps you met a colleague whom you'll end up starting another business with, or you got a PhD-level education in what it takes to build a team, or you simply learned more about what you're capable of outside your comfort zone.

The road to success is paved with failures.

Winners lose the most.

Oprah Winfrey was fired from her first job as an evening news reporter, told by her boss she was "unfit for television."

Michael Jordan didn't make the cut to play on his high school varsity basketball team. He was told he lacked the skills to play with the best guys.

J.K. Rowling was turned down by twelve publishers before finding a home for her first Harry Potter book.

What do all of these people have in common? They all possess a Possible Mindset. They weren't afraid to fail. But more important, when they did inevitably fail, they didn't characterize themselves as "Failures."

When you adopt a Possible Mindset, you'll stop letting your failures define you. Thomas Edison proved the importance of possessing a Possible Mindset when he was asked about his many initial failed attempts to invent the lightbulb. "I have not failed," he said. "I have just found ten thousand ways that won't work."

What if I told you that no matter what decision you make you can't fail? That each step you take will open the door to new possibilities? What perceived risks would you take on that you're currently afraid of?

The key to eventual success is something you have full and complete control over; it's all in the way you perceive your experiences, in the way you categorize and file your outcomes. Know that in any pursuit you'll either succeed or learn, and both are winning results.

I want you to remember this simple equation the next time you hesitate to take action out of fear of failure.

Failure + Perseverance = Success

KEY TAKEAWAY

Success is born from blood, sweat, and frozen tears
To unlock your best life, reframe your aversion to failure. You're going to fail sometimes, but there's no need to be afraid. To achieve great success, we need to learn and grow, and failure is essential to this process. Don't shy away from the sting of momentary setbacks. Resist the urge to give up when failure comes your way—instead, celebrate your failures as crucial building blocks to your eventual success. Most important, don't give up, press on.

HOW THIS APPLIES TO YOUR 12-HOUR WALK

The only failure is in not trying. It's nearly impossible to fail at the 12-Hour Walk, so let's take failure off the table and commit now. This is not a race. There are no world records at stake. As long as you engage in the process and commit to the full twelve-hour experience, you'll succeed. Along the way you'll strengthen your ability to persevere. As you prove to yourself that you *can* keep going for one more hour, one more mile, you'll learn that you have the capacity to persevere through any challenge.

WITH A <u>POSSIBLE MINDSET</u>,

I know that failures are the foundation of my success—winners lose the most.

Scan the QR code
or visit **12hourwalk.com/chapter7**
to view a short video that illuminates
the story from this chapter.

8

LIMITING BELIEF:
"I DON'T KNOW WHAT TO DO."

Intuition is a very powerful thing, more powerful
than intellect.

—STEVE JOBS

I was alone on an icy precipice in the depths of winter in
Pakistan at 23,500 feet on K2, the world's second tallest
mountain.

It was forty below—the kind of cold that lets you know what
it means to freeze to death. Ripping winds put the windchill at
minus-seventy, which made it tough to move, tough to breathe,
tough to even think. At these temps, your fingers and toes start
to feel like they belong to someone else, if you can even feel them
at all.

It was two-thirty in the afternoon. In a couple hours, without
the sun, the temperature would drop another twenty degrees.

K2 in "normal" summer climbing conditions is widely considered the world's most dangerous mountain—one in four climb-

ers who reach the summit fail to make it down alive—but I was a long way from normal. I was out to climb K2 in winter, a feat that had never been accomplished before this season. In some years, no one even tried, and yet this year there were a couple dozen climbers from several different teams on the mountain hoping to grab what the *New York Times* called "the last great prize of high-altitude mountaineering."

A prize like that . . . it spoke to me. Tell me something is out of reach, and I'll reach for it anyway, which explains how I came to be alone on that ledge in the Karakoram, battling the mighty K2, unable to take a breath without feeling as though I were being stabbed in the lungs by an icicle.

I'd gone ahead of my two Sherpa climbing partners through the Black Pyramid, a hugely complicated and exposed section of the Abruzzi Spur route. I'd been clipping my harness to old, frayed ropes from seasons past—an admittedly reckless move on my part, but climbing at this level is shot through with risk. The key is to take only calculated risks, and while I knew at that moment I was trusting my life to a ratty old rope, I also knew mixed in with the old ropes were a few sections of new rope that had been fixed by an all-Nepali team of heroic, world-class climbers who'd summited just two weeks earlier, becoming the first to climb K2 in winter and claiming the prize. And yet their success hadn't diminished my ambition to still reach the top.

Alarmingly, the rope I'd been following suddenly disappeared beneath the hard, windswept snow. I'd been counting on those fixed ropes, so I was stuck. I took a carabiner and clipped my backpack onto the end of the rope and sat down on it to protect me from the frozen ground while I figured out my next move. Despite the fierce winds, the sky was clear. I looked down the sheer face of the mountain into 8,000 feet of nothingness, all the way to the valley floor. One false step and I'd become the mountain's latest casualty.

If I pressed on, I'd be climbing blind—a terrifying thought in such gnarly conditions. But I wasn't without resources. I was still connected by radio and satellite to Base Camp, and to Jenna back home, and in the moment these two points of connection felt to me like even more essential lifelines than the fixed lines that had suddenly run out.

I unzipped the top of my backpack and pulled out my radio. I turned the knob to switch it on and the screen immediately went blank in the frigid air.

"Damn!"

I knew from experience in extreme cold that the only way to keep my devices functioning was to bury them beneath the several layers of my clothing, close to my body, so I'd taken the extra precaution of stowing my SAT phone against my skin. I reached for it and my heart leaped as it powered on, but in just seconds the cold caused that screen to go dark as well.

I'd never felt so alone—so utterly, chillingly alone.

My legs were trembling, probably due to some combination of cold and uncertainty. I hugged my knees and stomped my feet on the ice in front of me to keep the blood flowing. *Stomp, stomp, stomp* . . . like a soldier marching in place.

▲ ▲ ▲

My mind raced. The day before, my dear friend and climbing partner Dr. Jon Kedrowski had turned around not long after we'd left Base Camp. The mountain had been filling his head with dark, ominous thoughts. He'd been shaken by the passing of our friend Sergi Mingote, an accomplished Spanish climber who'd been at the midpoint of a years-long push to climb the fourteen tallest peaks in the world without supplemental oxygen. Sergi had fallen to his death on K2 a couple weeks earlier, just moments after Dr. Jon and I had rappelled the same section—a sad reminder that the mountain's fury would spare no one.

"This is dangerous shit, man," Dr. Jon had said, fighting back tears. "Something inside is telling me if I keep going, I'm going to die up there."

To Dr. Jon, the dangers were no longer acceptable. To me, they were part of the deal. I fully respected his decision to turn back—he might have been the only sane climber on the mountain!

"Colin," he said, "if you're feeling good, I still think you should keep going."

In that moment, so did I. And yet in *this* moment, cut off from the world, alone on this frigid, fragile slip of real estate, it felt to me like a winter assault on the angriest mountain on the planet was absolute madness, and for a long while I wondered what the hell I was doing up here.

I sat in this way for an hour and a half, until I saw a climber approaching from below. I thought it might be Ming Temba

Sherpa—a godsend because he was carrying some of our essential gear. But then I saw that it was Juan Pablo (JP) Mohr Prieto, a legendary climber from Chile. JP had been Sergi's climbing partner, and now he was determined to reach the summit to honor his fallen friend.

JP was perhaps the strongest climber I knew. He moved with a relentless precision that was unmistakable, even from a distance. We'd become close in the weeks following Sergi's death, waiting out a two-week storm while sharing the same dining tent at Base Camp, swapping stories over endless cups of tea. He told me about how excited he was to spend more time with his kids in the mountains as they grew up. I admired the hell out of him.

He was climbing without supplemental oxygen, and he was moving slowly, purposefully. I stood to embrace him. "Great to see you, man," I said. "Starting to wonder where everyone was. You okay?"

"My feet are so goddamn cold," he said in his accented English. "I am worried."

It was not like JP to acknowledge a vulnerability, but there it was.

I said, "We need to get to Camp 3 and get you warm, but the fixed rope ends here."

Camp 3, at roughly 24,000 feet, was the last camp before our summit push—and, mercifully, JP thought he knew the way.

"I'm pretty sure it's only a few hundred feet," he said, as I followed his gaze up the mountain. He continued: "We have our ice axes. We can climb this stretch un-roped, yes."

He was not asking, just stating the obvious—obvious to him,

anyway. The sheer drop-offs and large crevasses to either side of us would make climbing un-roped extremely dangerous; one false step would mean sudden death, but JP's certainty became my own. Before we could head out, however, we were joined on the slope by my climbing partners, Lakpa Temba Sherpa and Ming Temba Sherpa, as well as another lone climber, from Slovenia, named Tomaž Rotar.

I was used to being on my own in the most remote corners of the world, but this wasn't the time or place to be going solo, and as I set out with these other climbers I was overcome with a feeling of shared strength and purpose. The temperatures had dropped since I arrived on this slope a couple hours earlier, but I felt a little less cold in the company of these good men. We moved cautiously without the safety of the rope, skirting a giant crevasse, and made it to Camp 3 just as it was starting to get dark, just as the cold began to sap our resolve. We hurriedly dug two small platforms to accommodate my small three-man tent and JP's ultralight tent that was barely big enough for him, and then we squeezed inside to get warm.

Tomaž's camping gear was with his climbing partner, who was nowhere to be seen, so he took shelter with me, Ming Temba, and Lakpa Temba. It was a tight fit, but we made it work.

I tried to get the stove going, but the gas inside the canister was too cold to ignite. I went through a couple dozen matches but could not get a flame. I was beyond frustrated: the whole point of setting up camp at Camp 3 for a few hours was to melt a bunch of snow so we could hydrate, change into a dry pair of socks, and warm my SAT phone and radio so I could reestablish contact with Dr. Jon and Jenna before the planned summit push that night.

Next thing I knew, my friend Ali Sadpara poked his head through the tent flap and asked if he could come inside while he waited for his Icelandic partner, John Snorri Sigurjónsson, to arrive with their tent. I was thrilled to see him—and honored to take him in.

"He is an hour behind, I should think," Ali said. "I will make myself small."

There were now five of us squeezed in a three-man tent.

Ali was a fabled mountaineer, the Michael Jordan of Pakistan, a joy-filled human whose smile could fill even the coldest, most impossibly crowded tent with warmth and good cheer.

As we shifted to make room for him, he noticed me fighting with the matches.

"Here," he said, laughing, holding out his hands. "Let me."

I handed him the matches as he told me that when he made the historic first ascent of Nanga Parbat in winter, he'd learned to warm the metal gas canister *before* attempting to light the stove, and for the next little while he held a lit match to the outside of canister until the flame went out, and then again, and again, until the butane flowed.

"We got this, Colin," he said, smiling. He could have meant the stove *and* the climb because Ali was a buoyant soul who believed anything was possible. Either way, his smile told me what I already knew: the very best among us are always able to find light in the darkness.

Soon, there were a bunch of muffled, frantic voices outside our tent.

"You've got to be fucking kidding me!" I heard.

"I thought *you* had the tent."

"Shit, what the hell are we going to do?"

This was going from bad to worse.

Just then I felt the fabric of my tent shake, as a masked climber from another team unzipped my tent flaps and poked his ice-caked head inside. "Colin, is that you?" he gasped. "Can we come in . . . we have no tent, we'll freeze if we stay out here any longer."

Obviously, I couldn't let these people freeze, so I'd have to find a way to help get them warm, but it was a hassle and headache just the same—a situation that put *all* of us in jeopardy. The chaos and confusion that had been brewing outside was now mounting inside my small shelter.

Each time someone new asked to join us in our cramped space, I was hit by a rush of cold air that made it hard to think, hard to imagine heading back out into the night.

Ultimately, there were seven of us inside my three-man tent, with an eighth climber crouched in the vestibule by the front tent-flaps. We were wedged in so tight it was like we were jockeying for space in a crowded subway car.

When at last John Snorri arrived with Ali's tent, they set up just across from us, our front flaps practically touching. And the same predicament occurring in our tent now played out in their tent as the mercury dropped below minus-fifty degrees. Cumulatively, these two nylon cocoons were now providing emergency shelter for over a dozen desperate ice-caked climbers.

I checked in with Dr. Jon the moment I got the radio working.

"It's an absolute shitshow up here," I said. "We're smashed in so tight I can't even unzip my boots to put on dry socks." The others could hear me, but I didn't care. I needed to vent. "Who the fuck climbs to Camp 3 in the dark on K2 in winter without a tent? I'm all about helping each other out, but this is a nightmare for everybody."

"That sucks, man," Dr. Jon said, with a calm in his voice he was probably hoping I'd match.

"It more than sucks, man. I think people might die out here tonight," I yelled back frantically into the radio.

"Take a deep breath. You're in a tough spot, I get that, but your weather window is closing. You can still make the summit, but you've got to get out of your tent and go for it."

Next, I called Jenna to see if she could help me figure things out from back home. She'd trekked to K2 Base Camp with us at the beginning of the expedition, but had since returned home to Jackson Hole. I was happy to know she was a whole lot warmer and a whole lot safer than where I found myself. Her voice crackled through the SAT phone. As I strained to hear her, I could make out the hopeful voices from the other few tents on that snowy slope—cries of "We're going!" and "Let's do it!"

I held the phone out like an idiot, thinking Jenna could hear the sounds of pandemonium in and around my tent—not stopping to realize that she could barely hear me.

"What's your take on this situation?" I asked Jenna, clenching the phone close to my head again, needing her objective clarity.

"I don't have a good read on this one, Colin," she said. "This one's all you. Go, if you're going. It's time. Make the call. Now!"

For years, Jenna had been my eyes and ears at sea level—her "read" was my reality. I counted on her to help me track the countless details that informed every decision I faced while I was out on the edge, but this time I was on my own.

The call cut out and I sat there for a few long moments.

All along, I'd been hollering back and forth to Ali through our tents.

"What are you guys thinking?" I shouted when the call to Jenna cut out.

"We are thinking *go*!" Ali said. "Come with us, Colin. We shall make the top together!"

I appreciated Ali's positivity, but I couldn't embrace it just yet. I'd been thrown against the side of my tent, curled into a fetal position, trying to separate myself from the scrum of people. The packed conditions had left me unable to rest and hydrate the way I'd planned. I was stuck at a decision point—or, more accurately, an *indecision* point. Should I continue on with Ali and the others and claim glory if we succeed? Or should I head back down to join Dr. Jon in relative safety?

I closed my eyes, trying to tune out the chaos around me. I went inside myself, leaning on my years of Vipassana meditation practice, and what I found was the quiet of my own breath, the silence of my own thoughts.

What do I want? I asked myself.

I've got no idea how long I sat curled up like that. It could have been one minute . . . or twenty. I was rocking back and forth, whisper-chanting, "I've got to get home to Jenna and Jack. I've got to get home to Jenna and Jack." Over and over.

My wife . . . my dog . . . my family . . . my future.

Nothing else mattered.

One thing I've learned after a lifetime of pushing my body to its limits: the key to knowing when to press on is to trust my gut. When you know, you know. Here my intuition was telling me to play it safe, but before I could act on it, I did a quick ego check. After all, I was the guy who did hard things, relentless things . . . *impossible* things. I wanted to know how I'd feel if all these other climbers continued to the summit and made it safely back to Base Camp. Naturally, I'd be rooting for their safe return, but what would I tell myself if it turned out that my friends had the right stuff on this day when I didn't?

I visualized the scene to its best possible conclusion, all the way to what I'd say on their triumphant return: *That was insane. We were getting the shit beat out of us in those tents, but you went for it. I'm so goddamn proud of you, all of you.*

I crawled from my tent and poked my head into Ali's and said, "I'm not going."

He shot me a look like I was pulling his leg and said, "You are climbing so well, Colin. You were the fastest one through the Black Pyramid today. You are strong. The summit is ours!"

"My intuition is telling me to stop here and head back down at sunrise," I said. "I'm sorry."

I wasn't apologizing—and yet I was truly sorry.

"Well, you've got to trust yourself," he said. Then he smiled—that brilliant smile that could light up the night sky.

I grabbed Ali by the shoulders and brought him in for a half hug. I wished him well. Then I clambered outside and watched as the headlamps of my friends disappeared up the mountain into the night.

Ali Sadpara . . . John Snorri Sigurjónsson . . . JP Mohr Prieto . . .

▲ ▲ ▲

Those three men never returned that fateful night. It would be nearly six months before their frozen bodies were found. I was safely at home when that news reached me, and I hugged Jenna and Jack super close and wept. Even now, as I write this, it's impossible for me to accept the size of this loss.

An additional tragedy befell my friend Atanas Skatov—a celebrated Bulgarian climber who'd fallen to his death while descending back down the Black Pyramid from Camp 3 the morning after Ali, John, and JP disappeared. Atanas fatally fell just a half hour after I'd stood with him taking pictures together on our retreat back to Base Camp. Including Sergi, a total of five people died during my time on K2, leaving behind fifteen children to grow up without fathers. I didn't set out to climb with these good people, but they'd become dear friends over the course of that six-week expedition. Our shared experience—the coming together of our collective will—had fundamentally bonded us.

How do you make sense out of such an epic tragedy, such an overwhelming sadness? There is no sense in it, really. There is only coming to terms—something I'm still working on, frankly. And as I continue to process everything that happened, everything that *might* have happened, there is, in the center of the experience, a stark, shattering reminder that we need to trust our intuition.

Trust it, wherever it finds you, even if it's pointing you in a direction you hadn't initially considered.

Jenna summed it up best in an Instagram post she made on my account while I was still on K2, once she knew I was safe: "Our gut instinct, if we're willing to listen, can be the best guide in moments of uncertainty. Sometimes the hard call is the easy call."

HOW THIS STORY APPLIES TO YOU

When you know, you know.

Doesn't matter if you're on an icy ledge on K2 in the middle of winter, deciding if it makes sense to keep climbing—or lying awake on yet another sleepless night wondering if it makes sense to stay in a toxic relationship. Our life-and-death decisions aren't always about *life* and *death*, as they were for me on that mountain.

And yet, at their core, they are.

Choosing to share the rest of your life with someone who may or may not be right for you will determine the richness of your days going forward.

Weighing a move clear across the country for a new job, which requires you to uproot your kids from their friends at a vulnerable time in their young lives . . . also a big decision.

Continuing on in a business partnership that doesn't seem to be working out . . . that could lead to financial ruin.

The stakes can be just as high for you at sea level as they are at altitude, which is why it's so important to listen to your inner voice and trust your intuition, even when everyone around you is telling you to lean in some other way.

You know what you want. *You* know what's right for you. The big things in life . . . the little things in life . . . you know what will make you happy, what will drive you forward, what will hold you back. You know when to save your ass, and when to risk everything. Very often, you don't even need to think about it. You just *know*. You do. But many people aren't willing to listen to their own intuition when making important decisions. Instead, they second-guess themselves and fall into analysis paralysis.

You've probably been there at least once in your life. You feverishly write out an exhaustive list of pros and cons, but the list becomes so long you have no way to make sense of it. You ask all of your friends, family, and coworkers their opinions, but receive a litany of conflicting viewpoints. You get so stuck in your head that you resort to flipping a coin. Sad but true.

Ironically, before you took all these steps, deep down in your gut you already knew the answer.

Don't let overanalyzing, other people's opinions, or chance get in the way of your instinctive certainty.

One of the most dangerous rabbit holes people fall into when they're trying to listen to their gut is confusing what they hear with what they think is expected of them. What do I mean? Well, it's easy to talk ourselves into doing something because we believe that's what others want or need from us. That might mean participating in an investment your brother-in-law put together because you know he needs the funding, even though it's a lousy deal. Or going out drinking with a friend, even though staying in and getting a good night's sleep would be better for your morning workout.

When I was out there on the edge at Camp 3 on K2, jammed into that small tent like a sardine, it was difficult to separate what was right and good and true from what was expected of me—or, at least, from what I *thought* was expected of me.

The key is tuning out the noise in your "tent" and tuning into your Possible Mindset—so that you can listen to that calm voice within, telling you what you already know.

At the end of the day, *you* are the only one who knows what's right for you.

I'm reminded here of the ways we've come to rely on GPS technology to get us where we're going. When I first started driving, GPS didn't exist. If I came to a crossroads and didn't know which way to turn, I had to trust my sense of direction.

Our decision points are like that, don't you think? If we can't know with certainty which way to turn, we must fire up our internal Google Maps app and let it guide us. In the end, that's where all the variables and alternate routes and hazardous road conditions we're facing have already been stored.

You have the equipment you need. You have the information you need. The subscription on your internal GPS device has been paid in full.

There's tremendous power in knowing that you have the

answer—it's in your hard-wiring! Even if it pulls you from a hoped-for outcome. Even if it changes the way others might see you. Even if it takes you someplace entirely new.

Be clear on this: the big decisions in your life are on you—and *only* on you.

Because, hey, when you know you know.

KEY TAKEAWAY

Sometimes the hard call is the easy call
You think you don't know what to do. You have a big decision or question you keep asking yourself. Should I end this relationship or leave my job? Or maybe you think you're ready to have kids, but you keep telling yourself it's not the right time. Stop endlessly listing all the pros and cons. Rip off the Band-Aid. Make the call. You *do* know the answer. Let your intuition guide you.

HOW THIS APPLIES TO YOUR 12-HOUR WALK

The silence of this walk is my gift to you. Most of us are having an internal debate with ourselves about a big decision at any given moment. Take this opportunity, away from the chaos and distractions of the day-to-day, to mull it over, contemplate, and turn up the volume on your inner voice. Now that you can hear it loud and clear, trust what it's saying and take action.

WITH A <u>POSSIBLE MINDSET,</u>

I trust my gut. I *do* know the answer.

Scan the QR code
or visit **12hourwalk.com/chapter8**
to view a short video that illuminates
the story from this chapter.

9

LIMITING BELIEF:

"I DON'T HAVE THE RIGHT FRIENDS."

> You are the average of the five people you spend
> the most time with.
>
> —JIM ROHN

"We're gonna climb Everest, man!"

The words filled the air at the base of the mountain like a rallying cry. I turned toward the voice and saw a guy about ten years older than me, light brown hair, welcoming smile, dressed for a heavy-duty hike. He was bouncing up and down, beaming with excitement.

"I'm nervous," the guy said when we made eye contact. "How 'bout you? You good?"

I looked around at our picture-postcard setting and said, "Outstanding! Stoked to be here."

The guy stuck out his hand. "Marc Skalla," he said, with a Southern drawl. "My friends call me Skalla. Me and my buddy Paul here, we're from Atlanta." The guy next to him nodded hello.

"Colin," I said, shaking Skalla's hand. "Couple guys I just met, my tent-mates, they're also from Atlanta. Daley and Jeremy. You know them?"

"Haven't met everyone yet," Skalla said, "but yeah, there's a bunch of cool people here from Atlanta, I hear."

We chatted for a bit, waiting for Jesse Itzler to take the mic for some inspirational remarks to kick off our climb. I was huddled with a group of fellow climbers, about to head up one of the most storied mountains in the region. I looked around at the brilliant fall foliage decorating the mountainside in orange and rust and yellow and thought, *Everest never looked like this.*

▲ ▲ ▲

We weren't in the Himalayas but in the Green Mountains of Vermont, at the base of Stratton Mountain, where a couple hundred weekend warrior types had gathered to participate in the inaugural 29029 Everesting event—an endurance challenge that requires participants to climb 29,029 vertical feet, the equivalent of an Everest ascent from sea level, by lapping the same ski mountain trail over and over.

The event was the brainchild of Jesse Itzler and Marc Hodulich, who were on a mission to tap the wellspring of human potential.

Jesse is a force of nature—a relentless, effervescent spirit with an ability to make things happen. Early in his career he'd been a rapper and a record producer, then went on to co-found Marquis Jet and Zico coconut water, solidifying his reputation as a successful entrepreneur. He also happens to be a part owner of the Atlanta Hawks.

Marc is a force of nature himself, a former management consultant who has successfully developed and run a number of large-scale events and possesses a world-class talent for branding and marketing.

The two men had met through their kids, chasing them around town to birthday parties and flag football practice. In Marc's case the chasing was literal, Marc would run the four miles from his house to the field each week to coach his kids' practice, sparing himself the commute in a car. Jesse noticed Marc's unique habit and thought, *This is someone I should probably meet.*

Soon the two were talking about the tough challenges they'd taken on. Ultramarathons. Triathlons. Starting businesses. Raising a family. Turned out, like a lot of super-successful people, they were both always on the lookout for new opportunities.

"You ever thought of climbing Mount Everest?" Marc said to Jesse one night.

"Many times," Jesse said. "But I've got kids. Don't know that I can put myself out there like that, take on that risk."

It was an ordinary moment, just a couple dads shooting the breeze, but a switch had been flipped, and Marc and Jesse got to thinking that if they couldn't make the trip to Asia to climb Everest, maybe they could find a way to bring the summit to them.

"How high is Everest?" Jesse wondered, thinking out loud.

Marc googled it and said, "Twenty-nine thousand and twenty-nine feet."

"I can totally see it, man," Marc said. "It would be such an awesome endurance event, right? People could push their limits by climbing the same vertical feet as Everest, see what they've got, have a great time."

Jesse's big thing was to connect people from different backgrounds and put them together on common ground. "Think of the great community that could form on the back of something like this," he said. "Blood, sweat, and tears . . . that's how you build lasting friendships."

They continued to spitball.

"What if we got a ski resort to host the event in summer or fall?" Marc said. "People could climb up and down until they hit that 29,029 number."

"I love it!" Jesse said. "But climbing down, it'd be too hard on the knees. They'd need to ride the gondola down or something."

Together, they wondered who'd sign up for such an event, who might sponsor it, how much to charge for it . . . you know, the usual questions that swirl at the start of a new venture.

"One thing's for sure," Marc said. "Whoever comes out for something like this will be our kind of people."

▲ ▲ ▲

Not long after that my phone rang.

Jesse, Marc, and I knew each other by reputation. Several mutual friends, noticing a similar set of values and common interests, had encouraged us to connect. But we'd never met in person. That was about to change.

"We've got this idea for an event we're calling 29029 Everesting," Marc said enthusiastically as he went on to explain the concept.

He continued, "We're selling tickets to the general public. We've got some amazing folks already signed up. Like-minded souls that have the kind of passion and energy I love to be around. Our kind of people. You know what I mean?"

"Yeah. Totally," I said, smiling and nodding as Marc continued his pitch.

"Anyway, man, we'd love to invite you as a special guest to the inaugural event in Vermont. With your experience climbing the real Mount Everest, you'd add a lot to the group. So what do you think?"

"It's such a cool concept. I love it. I especially love the emphasis on camaraderie. Honestly, I've been struggling a bit to build community in this phase of life. I'm honored by the invitation. I'll be there!"

▲ ▲ ▲

As predicted, Skalla was *our* kind of people. We hit it off instantly.

"Tell me something," I said, as we stood there at the start line—Skalla burning off his nervous energy, me getting a feel for the folks who'd come out for this challenge. "What brings you here?"

"Been feeling a little lost," Skalla shared. "After seventeen years with a reliable routine, I've been navigating a career transition recently and I've been feeling really out of sorts. I've always dreamed of climbing Mount Everest. I've read every book about it. But, with two young daughters at home, now isn't the right time for me. But Everest in Vermont? I heard that and thought, man, that could really get me back on my game."

"Have you done a lot of endurance-type challenges?" I inquired, feeling his excitement to get started.

He laughed. "Not really, but I'm ready to leave it all out there on this mountain, and find out who I am on the other side of this."

Just then Eminem's "Lose Yourself," one of the all-time great pump-up songs, started blaring from the event speakers. Jesse stepped to the platform at the front of the crowd and went into his opening remarks, hyping up the group.

"Here we go, people," he told the participants. "You've got thirty-six hours to lap Stratton Mountain seventeen times. That's what it takes to climb *this* Everest!"

A word on the Stratton math: the trail beneath the gondola we'd be using for this event represented a vertical gain of approximately 1,700 feet. That meant we needed to hike the muddy, well-traveled mountain trail 17 times to "match" an Everest ascent. On average it would take roughly 90 to 120 minutes to complete each lap, including the ride down, which meant that if you climbed through the night, you'd have just enough time to achieve the goal in the allotted 36 hours.

Jesse concluded his hype speech with a line that has become one of the event signatures: "This isn't a race. This is you versus you!" He paused a second to let it sink in, then: "It's time to empty the tank out there. See what we're all made of."

We all let out a loud, raucous cheer, almost like a war cry, accompanied by a smattering of stand-alone shouts of "Woo-hoo!" and "Let's goooo!" and "Get 'er done, people!" I couldn't be sure, but it felt to me like no one was whooping it up louder than my new friend Skalla, who looked like he was itching to be let out of the gate.

Then Jesse led the group in a countdown—"Five, four, three, two, one . . . go!"—and as the air horn sounded to begin the climb, I clapped Skalla on the back and wished him luck.

"I'll see you out there," I said, as I began to climb. "Hope you find what you're looking for." And as I took my first steps uphill, it felt like I was on the path to finding something too.

▲ ▲ ▲

I paced myself on the first lap. Sure, I'd climbed Everest, but you don't climb from the bottom to the top of that Himalayan behemoth in one continuous push. This was a very different kind of challenge, and I didn't quite know what to expect. I surmised, however, that for a challenge this long it was probably best to start out with a simmer and build to a boil, keep something in the tank for reserve and not burn all my matches right out of the gate. One thing was clear straightaway: finishing 29029 was going to take some serious grit and perseverance. There was no shortcutting that kind of vertical gain.

Despite the grind, the atmosphere was electric.

Dance music blasted from the aid station halfway up the mountain and fellow participants chatted between labored breaths, continuing to climb together.

"One lap down, sixteen to go, Colin," a peppy, smiling volunteer called out as I unloaded from the gondola back at the base. She handed me some water and gave me a high five.

I didn't know how she knew my name. Then I looked down and remembered that my name was printed on my white participant bib. I laughed to myself. Still, the personal touch made it feel like we were all old friends out there.

"Make sure you brand the ascent board!" she called after me.

Before climbing up again, I walked over to a large wooden board engraved with all the participants' names, found mine, and burned the 29029 logo into one of the squares to record my first lap. I didn't realize it at the time, but this ritual would be hugely gratifying as the fatigue ratcheted up. Each brand marked one step closer to completing the challenge.

The next four laps passed by in a blur of muddy steps, grass stains, and cheerful camaraderie. I climbed with several different groups, discovering that each person had their own unique story as to why they were on the mountain.

There was a temporary tent city set up at the base to rest and store extra gear. We'd all been randomly assigned two tent-mates to share close quarters with for the weekend.

As the sun set, I quickly ducked back into my tent. Unzipping the flap, I was pleasantly surprised to run into Daley Ervin, one of my tent-mates. His big smile warmed an otherwise frigid canvas shelter.

"You taking a break?" he asked.

"No, just grabbing my headlamp before it gets pitch-black out there. You?"

"Same!" Daley replied. "Want to climb the next lap together?"

"For sure."

We headed off into the night, our breath visible in the cold air as we fell into an even stride. I quickly learned that Daley was no rookie when it came to endurance challenges.

"Wait, you rowed a boat across the Atlantic Ocean?" I said. I'd heard of ocean rowing, but at this point I'd never met someone who'd actually done it.

"How long did that take you?" I continued, peppering him with questions.

"Forty-five days. We broke the US pairs speed record," he replied, somehow managing to share the accomplishment with full humility.

My jaw dropped. "That's incredible, man. I'd love to row an ocean one day." A new seed was sown, and a new friendship was forming. We kept swapping stories of adventure as we labored uphill.

It was close to midnight. Methodically moving up the mountain were an array of headlamps, like an illuminated ant colony out for a stroll. It was chilly and the adrenaline surge I'd felt at the start line was petering out as the enormity of the challenge began to sink in. I could tell that everyone else felt the same way.

Not too far in front of Daley and me were two stationary headlamps hovering in the darkness, halted lights no longer progressing upward. As we approached, I recognized both illuminated faces. It was Skalla and his friend Paul. They were sitting. Paul clutched his right calf—not a good sign.

"I'm cramping pretty bad," Paul said, as we arrived on the

scene. "I'm only five laps in and there's twelve to go. Not even sure I can finish this one."

Daley could tell this guy was in a lot of pain—and as a veteran of many endurance-type events, he had a ready diagnosis.

"We've been sweating a ton," Daley announced. "Probably means you're low on salt."

He reached into the pocket of his running vest and pulled out some salt tablets. Then he handed them to Paul and said, "Take these. They'll make you feel better, then we can all finish this lap together, the four of us."

"You've got this! Stick with it. It's classic Type II fun, boys," I said, trying to rally our new friends.

Skalla looked back at me with a quizzical expression, "Type II fun? What's that?"

"Type I fun is fun in the moment. It's the kind of fun we normally think about, like dancing or skiing powder, maybe sunbathing. Don't get me wrong I love me some Type I fun, but Type II is really my favorite kind of fun and exactly what a challenge like this is all about. It's grueling when it's happening, but it becomes a life highlight in retrospect," I explained.

Daley chimed in, clearly knowing the concept too. "Before you know it, you'll be drinking a beer and looking back nostalgically at how you battled through this moment."

Reenergized now, both Skalla and Paul stood up. Skalla raised his fist in the air, motioned uphill, and exclaimed, "Type II fun . . . let's go, fellas!"

We all laughed at the absurdity of what we were attempting

but proceeded forward in unison like we'd known each other for years instead of hours. The deep kinship of our shared desire to complete the challenge propelled us upward.

Dozens of moments just like this one were playing out on the mountain, all through that night and into the following day. People were going out of their way to lend a hand, share some water, offer encouragement, show solidarity—shining a beacon of light more powerful than any headlamp. New friendships were forming all around on the back of shared struggles.

▲ ▲ ▲

I branded the ascent board for the sixteenth time. I could smell the wood burning as smoke from the brand rose upward toward my last square left to be marked. I hadn't slept all night. I was overtired and yet overjoyed that I had just one lap remaining to summit "Everest."

A volunteer took the branding iron from my weary hands. "Well done! Last lap . . . woo-hoo. You know what that means, Colin?" He paused for effect, then exclaimed, "*Red bib* . . . you earned it!"

He pulled out a red bib and handed it to me. My name was printed on it just like the original white one, but the red one showcased two more sweet words: "Final Ascent."

My legs were tired, my feet were covered in mud, my body caked with dry sweat. But despite all of that, there was something about that red bib that gave me the final boost of energy to climb the mountain one more time.

Participants riding down in the gondola recognized the red from above and shouted words of encouragement.

"You've got this, brother."

"Let's go, almost there!"

As I took my final steps to the summit of Stratton Mountain to complete my seventeenth lap and notch my first "simulated" Everest ascent to go along with my first "actual" Everest ascent, I noticed Marc Hodulich standing at the top cheering on each participant who came through. I'd had a memorable time climbing a couple laps with Jesse, his one-of-a-kind charisma and humor keeping our spirits high through the night as we battled to complete the challenge he'd helped dream up, but Marc hadn't been climbing. Instead he'd been running around juggling logistics behind the scenes all weekend to ensure the details of their vision went off without a hitch. It was heartwarming to see him on the summit taking it all in and adding to the positive energy of the moment.

He wrapped me in a bear hug as I reached the top.

"Congratulations. Well done," he said, smiling. "I know we don't have the same level of risk and lack of oxygen as the real Everest, but what did you think of the event?"

"Dude, this was one helluva weekend. Seriously, so much fun. It exceeded all of my expectations. The people . . . wow. What an inspiring group. I'm so glad you guys invited me," I said with genuine gratitude.

"Thanks, Colin. Thrilled to hear that. It seems like it's been a hit," he said, pulling me in for a second hug. Then he continued. "This first event was just a proof of concept. Honestly, man, we'd love for you to be involved in some way to help us grow the business if you're interested."

"One thing is for certain, Marc," I paused, "you and Jesse are my kind of people. I'd be honored to work with you to help expand this event series. But first, can I take a shower and a nap?"

We both laughed, relishing the joy of the moment.

I didn't immediately go to my tent to pass out; instead I stayed on the summit for hours cheering on the parade of red bibs worn by this new tribe of kindred spirits as the participants made their way to the finish line.

As I stood there, one woman crossed the finish line and immediately collapsed into the arms of two other climbers in red jerseys—friends she'd just made at the base the day before. She looked like she'd been through the wringer; sweat and tears running down her face and visibly exhausted, but you could tell from the look on her face that there was no place on Earth she'd rather be, and with no other group of people.

I walked over and patted her on the back. I could hear the deep satisfaction in her voice. "I did it," she said triumphantly, looking toward the sky. "I really, really can't believe I finished. I had so many doubts, but this community kept me going."

Daley and Skalla crossed the line together. We all hugged and soaked up the moment.

"Everest, baby!" Skalla exclaimed. "Wouldn't have made it without your support."

"We did it together," Daley said with a satisfied smile.

"Hell yeah, man. But I gotta be honest, I didn't know if I had it in me," Skalla said. "It's been a tough year."

"You know what? We should totally do Leadville together," Daley said. "This summer."

"What's Leadville?" Skalla wanted to know.

Daley told him about the Leadville 100, the famed hundred-mile ultramarathon trail race in Colorado.

"Hah!" Skalla said. "You've got the wrong guy. I tried to run a marathon once, in my twenties. About halfway through, my legs cramped up and I walked off the course."

"You've got it in you," Daley said. "We'll train together. You'll see."

Standing on that summit, I had a feeling this was just the beginning of a series of lifelong friendships. That feeling has been confirmed over the subsequent years. I count Marc, Jesse, Daley, Skalla, and several others I met that weekend in Vermont as some of my closest friends. Since then we've gone on numerous adventures together, supported each other through life transitions, and brought our families together to expand the tribe.

We didn't come out of that climb thinking, *Okay, we're done.* We came out of it thinking, *Okay, what's next? What more are we capable of?*

The answer lay at the heart of these new friendships.

HOW THIS STORY APPLIES TO YOU

It's simple really. You're the net product of the people you spend your time with.

We humans aren't solitary creatures. We thrive in the company of others—most of us, anyway. And yet we need to be in *good* company if we're to achieve our best.

Yes, it takes a village . . . to raise a child, pursue a goal, walk a purposeful path. But not just *any* village. If you surround yourself with people who consistently make poor choices, who are disappointed in their lives and careers and seem to be okay with that disappointment . . . well, then you'll probably end up just like them.

Conversely, if your community is filled with people who are always striving, pushing, reaching to improve themselves or their situations, you'll be inclined to do the same.

On the plane ride home to Atlanta from Vermont, Daley and Skalla made the commitment to each other to train for the Leadville Trail 100 Run. They made it a priority—and in making it a priority, they made a place in their lives for each other. Not only that, they recruited six other guys from Atlanta who'd also been at that first 29029 event to join them in this new challenge. They called themselves the Boundless 8, and their friendship knew no bounds after meeting that one weekend in Vermont.

You've probably heard a version of this phrase: "Hang around four millionaires and you'll probably be the fifth." In the same vein is the phrase "Hang around four criminals and you'll probably be the fifth."

You don't get to choose your family, but you do get to choose your friends. Absolutely, you do. And just as you choose to bring them into your life, you can choose to cut the cord if a friendship is no longer serving you.

Do you have an old friend from childhood who ticks all the wrong boxes for you? You meet them at the bar and catch up over a drink and you get excited and want to tell them good news about a promotion, an exciting trip, a new goal, but you're met with apathy or maybe even discouragement. It's soul-crushing.

Why do we spend time with people who don't celebrate our accomplishments and support us in our big dreams? What are we holding on to? If you can't share your good news with an old friend and count on getting back a supportive response, then it's time to swap out that old friend for a new one.

Step away from friendships that seem to be running on fumes.

OMG!

Look, this may sound harsh, but it's on me as your guide to lay down some hard truths, and as reluctant as I am to tell you to end a long-standing relationship, I know that, in certain cases, doing so is crucial if you want to live your best life.

You don't have to be *cruel* in the way you end things. Be grateful for the time you had with them but move forward and leave the past where it belongs. The beauty in letting go of old relationships that are dragging you down is that you're creating the space for new friendships that will help fuel your ambitions.

When I look back at the feats I've accomplished, I can see all the ways I've been empowered by the positive people in my life. They're the reason I've stood atop the world's tallest mountains and trekked across its most desolate landscapes. Even when they're not with me, at my side, they're with me in spirit. Their inspiration is the beneath-the-surface spur to live my best life.

Find the positive people in your orbit and let them be of service to you—as you strive to be of service to them. Seek out friendships that allow you to support each other, in success and in struggle.

After that inaugural 29029 Everesting event in 2017, Marc and Jesse offered to bring me on as a co-founder, to work beside them as business partners to grow and expand 29029.

Each time we host the event, what never fails to inspire me is the power of the community, the bonds forged, and the collective strength of a group of like-minded people taking on a unique challenge and supporting each other to conquer it.

The common characteristic that defines our community isn't world-class athleticism or God-given physical gifts. The common traits are grit, a desire to grow, and a passion to support others in becoming their best selves.

I've been deeply inspired by so many 29029 participants. I'll never forget the woman who arrived having never even completed a 5K. She showed up and stayed on the mountain for the entire thirty-six hours, finishing Everest just before the cutoff. Or the guy who lost 160 pounds while training to take on the challenge. Or the single-leg amputee giving it her all in the middle of a torrential downpour without offering excuses, or the woman whose husband had recently passed from ALS. She summited Everest in his honor.

In my opinion 29029 brings out the best in humanity and shows what anyone can accomplish with a Possible Mindset. These are the kinds of people I intentionally strive to surround myself with.

The key is finding *your* people—people who get what you're about and seem to share your values, interests, and goals. Whatever you're into, there are tons of people who are into the same thing. Seek them out. If you love to read, find a couple avid readers and start a book club. If crocheting is your thing, check out the bulletin boards at your local crafts store and pick a knitting group to join. If climbing the same damn mountain a bunch of times is what gets you going, sign up for one of our 29029 events.

I'm reminded here of the "crabs in a bucket" theory of human behavior. Do you know it? If you put several crabs in the same bucket, none will escape. The cast of crabs, collectively, will reach tirelessly with their claws to pull down any crab that's trying to escape. They're like those friends in our circles who are pulling us down. When we hold on to these broken relationships, we resign ourselves to the same bucket. We put a lid on our hopes and dreams.

If you've reached for this book, I'm betting you're out to take your life to a whole new level—but you'll never get there if you surround yourself with a bunch of crabs. Many people want to drag others down—but, fortunately, not everyone is wired that way. Find the right people and make them your people. As much as possible, build a community of friends who push you to grow and evolve.

To be clear, this isn't some theoretical exercise. It's essential work if you want to unlock your best life.

This applies to your online community as well. If you spend

any time on social media, you'll know what I'm talking about. Most of us follow people online who inspire us with aspirational pics and posts that influence us in a positive way. Fitness gurus, motivational speakers, celebrity role models, family and dear friends—there's a lot of powerful uplift to be gained from these individuals. But be leery of accounts that trigger you. The neighbor with the "better body" . . . the former colleague who is more often a source of jealousy than joy . . . the foodie influencer who's always having the "best meal ever."

Be honest with yourself about what inspires you and what pushes all the wrong buttons, and respond to that online audit the way you would to your real-life audit. Anyone who makes you feel bad about yourself, or doubt yourself, has no place in your social media feeds. If these people are triggering you, it's time to unfollow them. *Right now.* I'm sure your phone is somewhere within reach as you read this, so go ahead and reach for it. Click *unfollow*—see how good that feels!

No matter what your Everest is, you're more likely to achieve it if your community is the result of deliberate curation.

KEY TAKEAWAY

Beware of crabs
You're the net product of the people you spend your time with. The harsh reality is that as you curate your community to make room for the best, it will mean deciding which relationships are no longer serving you. Choose wisely since the decision regard-

157

ing who to keep and who to let go will have an outsized impact on who you'll become.

HOW THIS APPLIES TO YOUR 12-HOUR WALK

When you mention to your friends that you've put the 12-Hour Walk on your calendar for your own personal growth, take stock of who roots for you versus who tells you this is stupid, silly, or a waste of time. Although you'll be taking the 12-Hour Walk alone, know that there's a like-minded global community supporting you.

WITH A <u>POSSIBLE MINDSET</u>,

I have the power to choose friends who'll help me become the best version of myself.

Scan the QR code
or visit **12hourwalk.com/chapter9**
to view a short video that illuminates
the story from this chapter.

10

LIMITING BELIEF: "I DON'T HAVE ENOUGH TIME."

To achieve great things, two things are needed: a plan, and not quite enough time.

—LEONARD BERNSTEIN

"There's a ton of smoke over there, what's going on?" Dr. Jon shouted from the backseat of our rental car.

My face was unceremoniously smashed against the window glass. I'd just passed out in the front seat as Jenna feverishly drove us south through the wide expanse of mountains and desert of the Eastern Sierra. We'd left Boundary Peak that morning, just over the Nevada border, headed toward Mount Whitney, the tallest peak in California. I hadn't slept more than two or three hours per day over the past two weeks, and I was now in a perpetual daze as we raced across the USA, but Dr. Jon's words shocked me awake.

"Shit, that doesn't look good. The whole mountain looks like it's on fire," I exclaimed. "Jenna, how far are we from the Mount Whitney Ranger Station?"

Jenna glanced at her phone to check the GPS. She'd mapped out down to the minute every step of our journey across all fifty US states.

"It looks like we are forty-seven minutes out," she said.

My mind raced with all of the worst-case scenarios. *What if we can't climb? What if people are trapped in the smoke? If this delays us, are we going to run out of time to break the record?* So much had gone into arriving at this moment. I tried my best to remain calm, repeating one of my family's favorite mantras: *Don't bleed before you're cut!* Hopefully, we'd receive encouraging information once we arrived at the ranger station to pick up our climbing permit.

▲ ▲ ▲

Those forty-seven minutes felt like hours, but finally we pulled into the parking lot and ran inside. I approached the park ranger seated behind the desk. He was wearing the classic green pants, gray shirt, and wide-brimmed hat.

I tried my best to hide my desperation and nonchalantly said, "Hello, sir, we're here to pick up our Whitney climbing permit for today."

The red tape to climb Mount Whitney is surprisingly complicated. It's not only the highest peak in California but also the highest in the lower forty-eight states, and as a result the climb is in high demand. The Park Service strictly limits the supply of permits, so we'd entered a lottery six months earlier and been awarded this permit, for July 11, 2018, as our one and only shot to climb Whitney. The date also happened to be my dad's sixtieth birthday, and he'd trained all year back home on his organic farm in Hawaii to be in shape for this climb. He'd driven up separately to join us.

A lot was at stake.

The ranger looked up. "Have you taken a look outside?" he said without a hint of irony. "The Whitney trailhead got struck by lightning today. All that smoke is from an uncontained forest fire. It's bad."

"How bad? Can we still climb tonight? Is there another trail-head or something?" I interrupted the ranger, my anxiety rising. I must have seemed pretty pitiful.

He gave me an annoyed stare and continued, "Son, I don't know what else to tell you, Mother Nature is the boss out here. The mountain is closed, and there's no way of knowing for how long. Right now, the priority is on containment."

My heart sank.

"Sir, I've climbed to the highest point in thirty-nine states, all in the last fourteen days. I'm on pace to break the Fifty High Points world record, but if I can't climb Whitney it'll have been all for nothing," I shared, trying to generate some sympathy or at least provide some context to my situation.

"Thirty-nine states in fourteen days, how's that even possi-ble?" he asked. I could see his mind trying to crunch the numbers.

I went on to explain how Dr. Jon and I had reached the sum-mit of Denali on June 27, 2018, just two weeks prior. It was my second time on that breathtaking summit at 20,310 feet, the snowcapped Alaskan peaks glistening in all directions. The first time I'd scaled Denali's notorious slopes in 2016 I was racing to complete the final challenge that ultimately secured the Explorers Grand Slam and Seven Summits world records. This time I'd made the backbreaking ascent to start the clock on the "50HP" in a bid to be the fastest ever to reach the highest point in each of the fifty US states. The clock starts when you reach the summit of the first peak and ends when you reach the top of the fiftieth. Although 273 people had completed the 50HP challenge previously, most people took years or even decades to do so. I was hell-bent on measuring my time in days, not years.

We'd had the Denali summit all to ourselves that day. It was bitter cold, but clear and bright. Dr. Jon had looked at me, popping on his skis, and said, "Time's a ticking . . . let's gooooooo!" as he rocketed down the summit ridge.

Typically, Denali takes three to five days to descend—best-case scenario. But we didn't have that kind of time to spare. I had a plane bound for Hawaii to catch.

All told, just twelve hours after standing on the summit, we'd skied 13,000 feet down steep and technical terrain back to the base of "the Great One," awaiting a bush pilot to come extract us.

A low fog sat over the glacier at the base of Denali that morning, blocking any hope of a successful landing. We could hear the engine of the plane circling overhead, and with every second that ticked by my hopes of making it to Hawaii that day diminished. As if in a friendly wink from the Universe, the cloud cover opened briefly, illuminating a sliver of blue sky, and, as we gazed upward, our bush pilot, Chris, in an incredibly gutsy move, shot through the gap to scoop us up from the glacier.

The next sequence was a blur, emblematic of the following weeks. Jenna had put together a master class in logistics to turn our dream into a reality. But with so many moving parts and so many miles to cover, there was no chance the plan would unfold perfectly.

We touched down in Talkeetna, a small Alaskan town on the edge of Denali National Park. Ryan Kao, our 50HP videographer, was waiting on the tarmac with a rental car.

"Hop in! Sorry there's no time to shower, we've got to leave now if you want to make the flight to Hawaii," he said emphatically.

Although it was just me attempting to break the 50HP record, this project was a genuine team effort, and everyone was fully committed. Dr. Jon stayed behind to sort out our wet and stinking Denali gear; he planned to meet back up with me in a couple weeks so we could climb the toughest peaks in the West together.

After a frantic two-hour drive to Anchorage and full-out sprint through the airport terminal to our departure gate, Ryan and I were the last to board the plane. Less than twenty-four hours after standing on Alaska's highest point, we were airborne to Hawaii.

We landed in Kona, and tagged Hawaii's high point Mauna Kea, before heading directly back to the airport to fly back over the Pacific. Two down, forty-eight to go.

We made our way to Britton Hill in Florida—a 345-foot grassy mound beside a parking lot, a hilarious contrast to Denali—to meet the rest of the team, managing to summit the New Mexico and Oklahoma high points en route.

From there I tagged as many of the East Coast peaks as I could in rapid succession. We had the use of a private plane for a few key segments—supplied by my nutrition sponsor. In a single day we managed to rack up six state high points in the Southeast. But flying was not the norm. Primarily, Jenna and my dear friend Blake Brinker drove me thousands of miles in a thirty-foot RV, while I tried to catch up on sleep between peaks, bouncing around on the pullout bed at the back of the vehicle. There was no time for rest stops or hotel breaks. I was either climbing or in transit to the next high point, in constant motion twenty-four hours per day.

Constant motion, until Mount Whitney and this screeching halt.

After absorbing my longer than planned speech, the ranger wore an expression that suggested he'd softened some.

"Like I said before, none of us can do anything about Mother Nature's plan or this fire, but if you give me your phone number, I'll call you when the trailhead is safe and clear, and I'll honor your climbing permit on a new day if you make it back here."

▲ ▲ ▲

I knew full well that this fire could last weeks, costing me the chance of setting the 50HP record, but the ranger's word gave me a glimmer of hope.

Exiting the ranger station, I could taste the smoke. The mercury had climbed to nearly a hundred degrees on that dry California day. We—my dad, Dr. Jon, Ryan, Jenna, and I—all decided to huddle in the air-conditioning of my dad's motel room. Like a quarterback trying to rally the team on the final drive of the game, I tried to project confidence, but deep down the inevitability of defeat started to creep in.

"Okay, there's no way we're giving up after everything we've been through to get here. I want to hear everyone's best ideas."

Just then Jenna's phone rang and a quizzical look swept over her face.

"Hold on, guys, I have to take this real quick." Jenna stepped outside, but we could still hear her through the paper-thin motel walls. "Really, tomorrow?" she said, holding the phone to her ear. "Thank you so much, you have no idea how happy this makes me." She hung up and walked back into the room.

"You guys are never going to guess who that was," Jenna said, a devious smile emerging.

"Who?" we all shouted back nearly in unison.

"Arizona . . . the monsoon is here early, Humphreys Peak is now open! Colin, while you were pleading with the Whitney park ranger, I spotted a storm system on the radar near Flagstaff and started working on a new plan."

An extremely dry spring had led to officials closing public access to Humphreys Peak, the highest point in Arizona, due to high fire danger. Early monsoon rains in Arizona now meant that with the door to California temporarily closed, our luck had turned and another equally important door had just opened.

Jenna was at her best in moments like this. "Okay, I've

mapped out the new plan," she said, taking charge. "We've got to forget about Whitney for now. The pilots have agreed to fly us tomorrow to Arizona, but as we know, it's the last day we can use the private plane. Colin, I still want you to climb with your dad on his sixtieth birthday tomorrow; it'll just be in Arizona instead. Dr. Jon, I need you to take one for the team and drive Colin's dad's rental car four hours back to LAX tomorrow. We'll put you on a commercial flight to Denver. The rest of us will fly to Flagstaff first thing in the morning, and then I've arranged for Blake to meet us with the RV in Cheyenne, Wyoming, where we'll get dropped off after Colin and his dad summit Arizona. From there we should be able to drive through the night and hit Nebraska and Kansas by midnight, and meet Dr. Jon at the trailhead at Mount Elbert in Colorado at sunrise."

I looked around at everyone's face, as we each absorbed what Jenna had just laid out. I couldn't help but laugh, hysterically, at how ludicrous it all sounded. Yet I knew it was the only way to stay ahead of the ticking clock.

▲ ▲ ▲

With Jenna's plan in motion, my dad and I summited the highest peak in Arizona the following morning. We stayed at the top for only a couple of minutes, but standing up there, I pulled him into a hug and shared, "Happy birthday, Dad. I love you. Thanks for teaching me so much about the outdoors over the years." The former Eagle Scout smiled back.

As the wheels of the plane touched down on the tarmac of a small airstrip outside of Cheyenne, I could make out Blake's silhouette standing in front of our RV waving us in. I was thrilled to be reunited with Blake. Other than Jenna he'd been the closest person to me and my projects. Although his true world-class genius shines in the creative realm, helping me script speeches, build brands, and solve complex business issues, he wasn't too proud to get his hands dirty, and he'd answered the call when I asked him to drive the RV over two thousand miles from the East Coast to meet us. Nothing like having a loyal friend and confidant.

"Boy, am I glad to see you!" Blake said. "Welcome to Wyoming! Feels like it's been a lifetime since I last saw you in Portland, Maine." He chuckled and wrapped me in a big hug, his bearded grin smiling back at me. "Let's go!" he said, gesturing us into the RV.

The sun was setting as we raced across the Great Plains, hitting the Nebraska and Kansas high points through the night. Blake white-knuckled the steering wheel across dirt roads and winding mountain passes, eyes peeled for deer on the road, and after covering 620 miles over eleven hours, he shook me awake at the Mount Elbert trailhead in Colorado just after dawn.

"Bro, get up, it's time to climb again. Dr. Jon is here and ready to go."

I rubbed my eyes, still wearing my stinking climbing clothes from the day before. I grabbed my backpack from the floor and stumbled out the door of the RV.

"Welcome to my backyard," Dr. Jon exclaimed, arms held wide over his lanky six-foot-three frame. He'd grown up in Vail and was a proud Colorado native. He'd set numerous records on the state's storied 14,000-foot peaks. "This is an extra special climb for me today. It'll be my one hundredth summit of Mount Elbert." He wasn't kidding.

At 14,439 feet, Mount Elbert is no small climb. Back in the planning of this project I'd known this would be the start line of what we dubbed the "Western Ultramarathon." I'd climbed forty-two high points so far, in fifteen days, and aside from Denali, the eight remaining climbs constituted the hardest individual mountains of the entire 50HP project. I was tasked with completing them back-to-back-to-back if I wanted to claim the world record. Over the next week I'd attempt to tackle 150 trail miles and 50,000 vertical feet (the near equivalent of climbing Everest twice from sea level), not to mention travel over 4,000 miles between the peaks. On paper it looked like madness to pull all this off in the 168 hours of a single week. But madness or not, I was committed to giving it my best shot.

Dr. Jon and I took off from the Colorado trailhead on a bluebird summer day amid the stunning aspen groves. After topping out, we high-fived and jogged back down the trail. Turning to Dr. Jon while in full stride, I asked, "What do you think is going to happen with Mount Whitney? I have this sinking feeling we're going to do all of this and come up one short."

Dr. Jon possesses a laid-back optimism that I've learned to depend on in our years as climbing partners. "Don't worry about that right now, Colin. Let's just keep focused on each step. We'll find a way, I know it."

▲ ▲ ▲

The RV was parked at the trailhead when we returned. "Here, eat these, and let's roll." The engine was already running as Jenna handed us two sandwiches each and Blake nodded at us from the driver's seat, visibly exhausted from the lack of sleep. Ryan was doing his best to capture these moments on camera as we were all falling into a delirium from the nonstop motion.

"Okay, what's next? Utah, right?" I said in between massive bites.

"Change of plans!" Jenna replied, her smile growing. "Whitney is back on. The ranger just called, the fire is contained. We can use the permit if we get you back there tonight."

Before I knew it, we were racing down I-70 to the Denver airport. Jenna announced the next steps: "I booked flights for Dr. Jon, you, and Blake to LAX. There is a rental car under Blake's name. He'll drive you four hours to the mountain. Ryan and I will stay with the RV and meet you in Utah tomorrow after you've climbed Whitney."

By the time we arrived at the Mount Whitney trailhead, it was after midnight. We slammed the car doors and took off running up the trail, our headlamps illuminating the path. Through the open car window, Blake shouted a reminder: "I know most people take two days to climb Whitney, but Jenna booked us a flight out of Vegas this afternoon. You need to be up and down in eight hours tops. I'll be here waiting for you when you get down. It's a four-hour drive to the airport after that."

Just before sunrise we reached the infamous ninety-nine switchbacks that lead to the summit ridge. Dr. Jon recorded a

171

video of me walking in front of him. It looked like I was tripping over my own feet, like a drunk stumbling home from the bar.

In fact, I was falling asleep while walking—something I hadn't even known was possible. My eyes would involuntarily shut, body on the verge of collapse, and then I'd catch myself in a jolt just before falling to the ground. We'd been going nonstop for seventeen days.

▲ ▲ ▲

That was the state of affairs as we made our way up and down Mount Whitney in time to link up with Blake in the parking lot, speed across Death Valley to Las Vegas, catch our flight to Salt Lake City, and meet Jenna and the RV to take us to Utah's Kings Peak that night.

Kings Peak isn't a technical climb, but it's far—nearly thirty miles round-trip. My childhood best friend Lucas Clarke had driven up to join us, and he added a much-needed boost of energy. As we left the trailhead again at midnight, Lucas shouted, "Let's go, boys . . . just a casual marathon through the night, we got this." I locked eyes with Dr. Jon, not needing to speak to convey what we were both thinking: *This is insane!*

I wish I could tell you what happened that night, but as I try to recall it's all just a jumble of trail miles, and a sunrise summit photo to prove we made it to the top.

"Forty-five down, five to go," Jenna said, greeting our weary bodies again with food and positivity, as we piled back into the RV. "But as you guys know, this next one is the longest. Gannett Peak in Wyoming is over forty miles round-trip, and you'll need your crampons, ice axes, and rope for the summit glacier." She paused, hesitating to tell us the next detail. "It's only a three-hour drive from here, so try and sleep, it's a quick turnaround."

Sleep didn't take much trying at this point. As soon as I sat down, before the RV engine roared to life, I was out cold, the crumbs of my sandwich indelicately spread over my lap.

Fourteen hours into our nonstop assault on Gannett Peak (the standard itinerary takes five days), Dr. Jon and I reached the base of the glacier and it was time to strap on our crampons. Due to the distance of the approach, I'd chosen to wear light trail shoes that weren't crampon compatible. I figured I could make do, jury-rigging a solution.

Bad idea.

A few hundred feet up the glacier I watched in terror as my crampon dislodged from my shoe and went skittering down the steep face, stopping just inches before disappearing over a huge cliff. Thankfully, Dr. Jon was able to retrieve it. He had a spare roll of white athletic tape that we used to secure the crampon back onto my shoe. My foot looked like a mummy from a third-rate horror film. We both knew this was quite unsafe and precarious, but I didn't see another choice. And quitting was certainly not an option.

"I hope that holds," I said with a slight grin, and proceeded to climb toward the summit.

Thankfully, hold it did, and over the next thirty-six hours we ticked off Gannett Peak in Wyoming, Borah Peak in Idaho, and Granite Peak in Montana. The latter was another climb that typically required multiple days and technical vertical–rock climbing skills to complete. We scaled the mountain in a punishing fifteen hours between lightning storms.

▲ ▲ ▲

Stumbling back to the trailhead after summiting Granite, I could barely process what Jenna was telling us. "Two more high points to set the world record, Colin—but to get you up Mount Rainier tonight, we have to get crafty with the logistics one last time." She continued, "I've booked you a commercial flight out of Bozeman to Seattle in a few hours. Blake will drive you from Sea-Tac to the trailhead. It'll be a fifteen-hour slog for me and Ryan in the RV, but we should be able to make it to Washington by the time you're descending, and we'll all drive together to the final summit in Oregon."

That night, less than a week since we'd begun the "Western Ultramarathon" in Colorado, Dr. Jon and I took off up the Muir snowfield on Mount Rainier. With its bottomless crevasses and avalanche danger, Rainier is a classic proving ground for local mountaineers. I was born just an hour down the road, in Olympia, Washington, and having grown up in the Pacific Northwest, I'd climbed this peak numerous times, as had Dr. Jon.

Around 3 a.m., while rock hopping across a creek, Dr. Jon turned to me and said, "I'm going to fill up my water here, you go ahead. I'll catch up to you before we need to rope up."

I nodded and kept climbing up the snowfield, the moonlight silhouetting the rock towers and glaciers above. Two more hours passed. I reached the technical section where we needed to rope together for safety, so I turned around, imagining through the night that Dr. Jon had been right behind me. But as I looked back there was no sign of him. No headlamp, no shadows, no footprints. Nothing.

I was alone, and confused.

Dr. Jon knew this route as well as anyone; he couldn't have gotten lost. I leaned up against a boulder to ponder my options, and after about an hour, the first light started to permeate the sky. I squinted and thought I could make out a figure moving upward, but it was 2,000 feet below. *Could that be him? How did he end up so far behind? It will take an hour or two for him to reach me,* I thought.

All I could do was wait.

As the figure approached, I could tell by his gait that it was undeniably Dr. Jon. I was relieved but still confused.

I shouted down to him, "What happened? Are you okay?"

His gregarious laugh echoed up the slope. "Sorry, man, I sat down to fill up my water, and woke up two hours later facedown in the snow." I could see his goofy smile approaching, and with a wink he said, "Don't worry, I'm well rested now after that nap. Let's rope up and hit the summit."

Hit the summit we did, albeit in our exhausted state moving a bit slower than our normal pace.

▲ ▲ ▲

Only one high point remained, in my home state of Oregon.

Road weary but chipper, Jenna met us with the RV after her long drive from Montana, and as a team we drove the familiar evergreen forest roads of my childhood to Mount Hood. From the day we'd started dreaming up this project I'd visualized this moment, returning home—ahead of world record pace—to the mountain where I'd first learned to climb.

One last time Dr. Jon and I left the RV in the dark of night, to climb toward Oregon's snowcapped summit. Halfway up Dr. Jon turned to me and said, "I love you, brother, but this is your project, this one's all you, you've got this. I'll wait for you down here. Go stop that world record clock!"

I wrapped him in a tight hug, our down jackets smashed against each other. "I never could have done this without all your help. This is just as much your record as it is mine."

With a blanket of stars overhead, I reached the familiar summit slopes alone a few hours later.

"Suuuuummmmmiiiiiittttttt!" I yelled into the crisp night sky, grabbing my GPS one last time to mark the spot and stop the clock.

Over thirteen thousand miles traveled, all fifty US state high points climbed in a new world record time of twenty-one days, nine hours, and forty-eight minutes.

Then I reached down into my backpack and pulled out my ultralight sleeping bag, crawled inside, and fell into the deepest sleep right there on the summit.

HOW THIS STORY APPLIES TO YOU

Time is our most precious resource.

Let me ask you a random question. Have you seen all seventy-three episodes of *Game of Thrones*? What about every episode of *Tiger King* or *Yellowstone*?

If you're like most people (myself included), your answer is: Yes!

Were those shows entertaining as hell? Sure. Were they essential to living your best life? Probably not.

Too often I hear people say things like "I don't have enough time to work out" or "I don't have enough time to learn a new skill" or "I don't have enough time to work on new goals."

So let me get this straight, you've watched over seventy hours of *Game of Thrones*, but you don't have time to go to the gym or passionately pursue your dreams?

Reality check: you *do* have plenty of time, you're just not prioritizing your time effectively.

There are 168 hours in a week. How many hours do you spend scrolling social media? How many hours do you spend watching mindless television? How many hours do you spend daydreaming about living a more fulfilling life?

I've fallen victim to these time-sucks myself. I'm far from perfect.

However, when I look back at my proudest achievements, there's one thing they all have in common. In pursuing them, I cut out the unnecessary to focus my time and energy on my goals and passions. Time is our most precious resource. With a Possible Mindset, you'll become intentional in how you spend it.

I shared the story of 50HP with you as an example of what's possible in a limited amount of time. If I can reach the summit of fifty peaks in fifty states in three weeks, I have no doubt you can reprioritize your weekly schedule to make room for the things that really matter to you.

I'm not suggesting that you ditch everything to spend all of your time on something completely different (unless of course that's the kind of dramatic shift you need). Rather, I'm asking you to make bite-sized adjustments to your daily schedule to optimize the quality of your time.

Take a second to pull out your phone and look at how much screen time you've succumbed to this week. I'm not going anywhere, go ahead and look. Let's do a quick time audit.

The average person spends about five to six hours per day on screens not related to work. Five to six hours per day! Imagine what you could do with your life if you took just two of those hours away from the screen each day and instead invested them in your health, your goals, your relationships. Two hours per day multiplied by seven days equals fourteen hours per week. That's sixty or more hours a month, and over seven hundred hours per year.

In seven hundred hours you could become fluent in a new language, become the healthiest you've ever been, create new memories with your family, work on that side hustle you've always dreamed about, or read a hundred books!

The time is now to take back those hours and prioritize what really matters to you.

But what really matters?

One of the biggest mistakes I see people make is not prioritizing their own self-care. We fill our days with work, meetings, to-do lists, and childcare, forgetting to allocate any time to ourselves.

We're told if we do set aside some "me time" that we're selfish.

Our justification for making this sacrifice is that we want to get ahead in our careers, or always be there for our kids. On the surface there's a logic to that. These are worthy aspirations. However, I've come to realize that continually sacrificing self-care leads to burnout, which, ironically, makes us *worse* at the things we're sacrificing for in the first place. We become worse at our jobs, less patient as parents, distant from our spouses, and generally unhealthy and unhappy.

Think about it: when we work an hour less so that we can exercise, we become more productive and efficient at our jobs. When we turn off the TV and instead get an extra hour of sleep, we wake up refreshed and are more present with our kids. When you're the best version of yourself, it's a net positive for everyone.

Prioritizing self-care is, in fact, *selfless*.

The next time you find yourself saying "I don't have enough time for myself," stop right there. Take a deep breath and remember that prioritizing self-care is a vital step toward living your best life.

The truth: you *do* have enough time for yourself. But you have to seize it.

Let's zoom out a bit.

It's human nature to block out the inevitability of death, and tell ourselves there'll be more time for this or that in the future.

Let's say you're forty years old. The average life expectancy in the United States is roughly seventy-eight. So, on average, at forty you have more years behind you than in front of you.

Let's say your parents live on the other side of the country and they're seventy years old. How many times do you see them per year? Twice maybe—once for the holidays, and once more for a long weekend.

If that's the case, you have only sixteen more visits with your parents *ever* before they pass. I know, it's easy to get bummed out by that—but that's not the point.

The point is that time is *finite*. Make sure that every day, every week, every month, every year, you spend it wisely.

KEY TAKEAWAY

To reach your "high points," spend your time wisely
Time is not your enemy, it's your most precious resource. Take stock of what's on your calendar, and make sure that your time is allocated to things that have maximal benefit. Your "best life" calendar is not full of to dos, have tos, and shoulds, where you feel like a slave to time. Your "best life" calendar *is* full of get tos and want tos, quality events that fill your cup and help you grow, build, and refresh. Cut out the unnecessary time-sucks, and replace them with soul-filling agenda items. There are 168 hours in every week. Make them count.

HOW THIS APPLIES TO YOUR 12-HOUR WALK

Avoid falling victim to the most common excuse I hear about the 12-Hour Walk: "I don't have enough time." Unshackle yourself from that mindset. Book the babysitter, use a vacation day from work, skip a Sunday of watching football. Bottom line: put it on your calendar and make it a priority. Your best life awaits on the other side of this walk. This twelve-hour investment in yourself will ultimately save you tremendous amounts of time in the future, as you'll begin to optimize and prioritize your time more effectively. Remember, self-care is selfless, not selfish. You'll be a better parent, spouse, neighbor, friend, and employee having invested the time in yourself and taken the Walk. You can't afford not to.

WITH A <u>POSSIBLE MINDSET</u>,

I have enough time and I spend it wisely.

Scan the QR code
or visit **12hourwalk.com/chapter10**
to view a short video that illuminates
the story from this chapter.

11

LIMITING BELIEF:
"I DON'T HAVE ENOUGH MONEY."

If you look at what you have in life, you'll always have more. If you look at what you don't have in life, you'll never have enough.

—OPRAH WINFREY

I stood balanced on the toilet seat so that if anyone came into the bathroom they couldn't see my legs under the stall doors.

My heart raced like I was a bank robber trying to make a clean getaway.

Truthfully, the stakes were much smaller, though to my seventh-grade brain it felt like life and death.

I'd just stolen a bottle of Wite-Out from my teacher's desk drawer.

I looked down toward the toilet bowl in embarrassment at my grass-stained and scuffed white Jack Purcell Converse sneakers. My face was still flush from the humiliating exchange earlier in the hallway when my middle school crush asked me,

"Why are you wearing those dirty shoes? You need to throw those out and buy a new pair, they're cheap anyways. Jacks aren't cute unless they're all white," she said with authoritative conviction.

I was desperate to fit in, but buying a new pair of shoes was not an option. Before the school year I'd begged my mom for a new pair of Jack Purcells. I remember my relief when we found them on sale at Payless ShoeSource for $32.99. At the checkout counter my mom handed me the Converse shoe box and said, "You have to take care of these and make them last. We don't have any more money for new shoes until next year." Then she mumbled under her breath, "And let's hope your feet don't grow too quickly this year."

At the job of keeping those Jack Purcells clean and pristine I'd proven woefully inadequate. So here I was, crouched down, unscrewing the top of the Wite-Out bottle and methodically painting the dirty canvas. As I worked to apply the goop evenly, I prayed that none of my peers would notice the crude fix.

▲ ▲ ▲

To be clear, as a kid I always felt secure that I'd have a roof over my head and food on the table, even if that food was free samples from the hippie natural foods store that my parents both worked at. But, overall, money was tight. My parents were in their early twenties when they had my sister and me. They both worked full-time; my dad worked nights and weekend shifts, and my mom worked during the days. They alternated their schedules so that one of them could be home with us kids, since daycare wasn't an option with their limited paychecks. The logistics of making ends meet left little time for them to invest in their marriage, and when I turned ten they divorced.

Growing up, I don't remember traveling on airplanes other than the couple of times my grandparents bought us airfare to Chicago to celebrate Christmas with them. However, that didn't stop us from having a multitude of adventures. Our adventures just happened to be closer to home, but I hardly knew the difference. My formative years were spent exploring the wild places of the Pacific Northwest.

"The outdoors are free," my dad would say, loading up the old blue-and-wood-paneled family minivan before driving us to a state park or campground near our house in Portland, Oregon.

What my parents lacked in resources they made up for in passion and creativity. They instilled in me a belief that if you want something bad enough and are willing to work hard for it, nothing is out of reach.

One day, when I was fourteen years old, my stepdad, Brian— whom my mom had met while working in the natural foods industry—came into the family room and said, "Come on, kids, jump in the car, there's something we want to show you." We were all thrilled because it sounded like an adventure was coming our way. And in hindsight, that was truer than I could've ever imagined.

My mom and Brian navigated the rush-hour traffic and pulled into a strip mall on the outskirts of Portland. My sisters and I unloaded in the sparse parking lot. "You see that building right there?" Brian said, pointing to a somewhat disheveled commercial property. "We've decided to take our life savings and build a natural foods grocery store chain. We're going all-in on our dream. Our first store will open right here."

After years working their way up in the grocery industry, from hourly shift work to management, they had a vision for a better natural foods concept. They were convinced that their idea was a way to save the planet, and they threw around words like "local," "organic," and "sustainable" long before most people knew what they were talking about.

The sparkle in their eyes that day, dreaming about what they could create, left a massive impact on my fourteen-year-old mind. They gazed at that old building like it was the Taj Mahal.

My family dinner table conversations during high school were like taking Entrepreneurship 101. Balance sheets and sales forecasts were spread out on the kitchen counter. Every evening was seasoned with business planning as my mom and Brian bounced ideas off each other. We'd hear things like:

"The brand should be built on uncompromising commitment to customer service."

"Can we afford another full-page marketing insert in the *Oregonian* this week?"

"We should look at the new sales forecasts before tomorrow."

On and on it went.

I witnessed the stress involved in deciding how many turkeys to purchase for the Thanksgiving rush, and I learned the detrimental effects of not selling-through a store's perishable inventory. I watched as my parents' daring idea slowly came to life. The many ups and downs of committing fully to a dream were laid bare.

▲ ▲ ▲

It was probably no coincidence then that fifteen years later, in 2015, Jenna and I walked into a creative agency in Portland with a $10,000 check, ready to risk our entire life savings to chase our own dreams.

I'd recently asked Jenna to marry me. With the blissful naivete of a recently engaged couple, we looked out from the mountaintop where I'd gotten down on one knee, and we asked ourselves, "How do we want to spend our days? What could we build and create together that would be fulfilling and meaningful?"

With the realization sinking in that I was going to fail in my attempt to make the Olympics in triathlon, I wasn't fully prepared to give up on my passion for athletic pursuits. During our post-engagement brainstorm I asked Jenna, "I still want to push my body, maybe even pursue my childhood dream of climbing Mount Everest, but do you think there's a way to pair that with a purpose larger than ourselves?"

It was that adventurous spirit that landed us at this creative agency. We were ushered through the glass doors of a stylish conference room. The walls were covered in iconic graphics, global Nike campaigns and other high-profile projects, a nod to the prominent clients the agency had worked with. Seated around a table were a number of top-tier web developers and digital creatives.

Taking a deep breath, I began. "Imagine climbing to the summit of the tallest mountain on each of the seven continents. Imagine trekking to the North and South Poles. Very few people have ever visited these places, even fewer have reached all of them by completing what's known as the Explorers Grand Slam." I tried to project confidence, since this was the first time I'd explained my dream to a roomful of strangers.

I continued, "Only about fifty people have completed the Explorers Grand Slam, and usually they take a decade or longer to do so. My aim is to set a new world record by completing all of the expeditions back-to-back in just four months, next year."

A few eyebrows rose around the room as Jenna jumped in: "But our larger goal is to use the media exposure from this project to build a platform so that we can start a nonprofit that inspires kids to dream big, set audacious goals, get outside, and live active and healthy lives." I smiled, thinking about how influential my time in the outdoors as a kid had been.

"So what's this all going to cost?" the red-haired, skinny-jean-clad creative director asked, half-skeptical, half-intrigued. "I can't imagine the logistics involved in getting to all these far-off places is cheap."

"For the hard costs alone we need to raise $500,000," I said, trying unsuccessfully to regain my poised tone. Clearing my throat, I went on, "But we only have $10,000 to our names, so we're hoping that you can help us build a professional website and brand, so that we can pitch this idea to potential sponsors."

Mr. Hipster nodded and looked at his colleagues disconcertedly before he uttered a low-energy and rather clinical "I see."

Not quite the response we were hoping for. We quickly learned that our $10,000 life savings didn't buy you much at an agency of this stature, but we left the meeting with a handshake at least. Thankfully, the creative director took pity on us and agreed to help support our mission.

Back in the parking lot afterward, I unlocked the door to our old rusted Subaru. I was second-guessing myself. "Jenna, what if nobody wants to sponsor our project? We just promised those guys all our money."

She laughed nervously, winking at me, "Well, at least we'll have a cool website."

▲ ▲ ▲

BEYOND 7/2 was the name we settled on for our project's brand and nonprofit. Late one night, Jenna cleverly came up with a design for the logo, turning the "7" into an ice axe. The "7" stood for the Seven Summits, and the "2" for both poles. We'd hoped the word "Beyond" was powerful enough to project the impact we were striving for.

Website and marketing materials in hand, we hit the streets searching for funding.

I woke up each morning over the next six months and

cold-called companies, internet-stalked potential contacts on LinkedIn, and pitched every person who'd listen, chasing loose connections to companies or brands that I thought might want to sponsor the project.

Nothing.

It seemed like every step led to another dead end. The flashy website was little help.

Most of the time I couldn't even persuade anyone to take a meeting, and the times I did actually convince someone to hear my pitch I was met with the same response to my final question, "So do you think this is something your company would be interested in sponsoring?"

"No."

Or a variation on that, "Good luck, kid," which I came to realize was just a thinly veiled and slightly more polite way of saying, "No." We must've heard a hundred versions of no during those long months.

Trying to remain optimistic, we initiated our first round of nonprofit outreach and started visiting elementary schools in the area. We shared the Grand Slam plan and invited teachers to embed expedition content into their curriculum in partnership with the project. In our vision, they would teach lessons about geography, history, culture, and climate in unique ways as students followed my expedition in real time.

As the date of my scheduled departure neared, I found myself standing in front of a class of second graders. The room was buzzing as I answered questions from curious students about penguins, polar bears, and whether I might meet Santa at the North

Pole. I loved the students' unfiltered enthusiasm, but standing there, knowing I was well short of raising the funds I needed to actually *attempt* the Grand Slam, I began to feel like a fraud.

If I don't find sponsorship soon, I'll have to cancel this whole thing, I thought, feeling defeated.

▲ ▲ ▲

The following week, at a coffee shop near our house, I ran into a friend named Angelo, who said there was somebody I should meet. Angelo, who knew the troubles Jenna and I were having launching our project, attended Sunday morning spin classes, and this person, he said, was also a regular.

"She was a big-time runner in the past—a world record holder. Might lift your spirits. Anyway, you should come and meet her," he said.

The following Sunday I dragged myself to the gym by my house. After years competing as a professional triathlete, my ego got the better of me. *Exercising in a group fitness class is beneath me*, I reasoned. But I was desperate and figured I had nothing to lose.

As I was raising the seat on my spin bike, Angelo walked over and pulled me toward the side of the room, where a woman was already riding hard even though the class hadn't started. She looked to be in her mid-fifties and was lean and amazingly fit. Sweat glistened on her arms and neck, and I had the sudden realization that spin classes had real athletes in them.

"Colin, this is Kathy. Kathy, Colin."

Kathy paused from her workout and we shook hands.

"Kathy broke the world record for the 5K in the 1970s," Angelo said. "Kathy Mills then, collegiate legend."

"Million years ago," Kathy immediately said, grabbing a towel and shaking her head as though it wasn't that important. "So what's this project Angelo has told me about?"

I took a breath. I'd told the story hundreds of times by then in meetings, coffee shops, bars, schools, even in the street when I'd meet some old acquaintances, and though I knew I'd probably gotten better at it, the lack of success had started to nag at me. Maybe I wasn't doing it right.

But as I opened my mouth that morning, it all came together and flowed out, both the passion and the clarity. I already instantly admired Kathy, but I wasn't *pitching* her, wasn't *asking* anything of her, and that was probably the difference. I was just a guy in a Sunday morning spin class talking about his dreams and goals.

And then for the next ninety minutes I spun. It was a fine workout, better than I'd expected, and when it was over, I wiped off my bike and walked over to say goodbye to Kathy. A guy was toweling off next to her.

"This is my husband, Mark," Kathy said. He was about her age, with salt-and-pepper hair, a lightly stubbled chin, and the look of a former athlete. "Tell Mark the thing you're working on, Colin," she said, as he and I shook hands.

So the story poured out again, distilled down and simplified. Around us, people laughed and wiped off their bikes as they chatted and packed up their stuff. And it felt like the story—the dream that Jenna and I had crafted so carefully—had in a strange way become bigger than we were. In all the other more formal meetings and presentations, I realized, even as I stood there talking, that I'd been trying to force it, make something happen. Now I just conveyed my passion with no expectations whatsoever.

When I was done, Mark immediately nodded. "I like this," he said. "And I think it fits in really well with some things we've been doing at the company I work for."

"Great," I said, happy to hear any kind of welcome response, but expecting nothing to come of it. I'd heard too many people say similar things and then add "good luck, kid" at the end.

"Here, let me get you a card," Mark said, bending over and rustling through his gym bag. "Send me an email and a link to your website if you have one and we'll talk."

I held it in my sweaty hand, staring down at it.

"Mark Parker," the card said. "Chief Executive Officer, Nike, Inc."

HOW THIS STORY APPLIES TO YOU

So what do you think? Did I just get lucky?

Was it pure luck to be in the right place at the right time to land a Nike sponsorship—one that amplified our nonprofit mission while allowing me to realize my dream of climbing Everest en route to setting my first two world records for the Seven Summits and the Explorers Grand Slam in 139 days?

My answer: no.

One of my mom's favorite sayings is *Luck comes to those who are prepared*.

The success of this story wasn't based on luck, but rather on perseverance and an unwavering belief in a positive outcome— *despite* having the first hundred people I pitched slam the door in my face.

In the following pages I'll show you how you can use a Possible Mindset to realize your dreams, how money is abundant and you can have it too.

Recently, I polled my Instagram audience, asking "What's the number one thing standing in the way of you living your best life?" Over 75 percent of the answers were the same: "I don't have enough money." Well then, if so many of you have the same perceived roadblock, let's talk about how you can conquer this limiting belief.

Earlier in this book I asked you to embrace discomfort. So it's only fair that I take my own advice here and step out of *my* comfort zone. These following paragraphs are uncomfortable for me to write, but I share them to illuminate an important point.

Get ready to cringe.

Jenna and I have turned that initial $10,000 investment in ourselves into significant financial success over the years. We've built numerous highly profitable business ventures centered on speaking, publishing, branding deals, as well as film and television projects in Hollywood. In addition, my business partners and I had an eight-figure exit from selling our events company.

The point is: I don't have to use Wite-Out on my sneakers anymore.

Does talking about finances, either mine or yours, make you feel uncomfortable? Why *is* that?

The answer: we've been told, overtly and subconsciously, our entire lives that we shouldn't talk about money—that money is an off-limits taboo subject. Yet the vast majority of us spend our waking hours wishing we had more.

And therein lies the problem.

Society has programmed us to believe so-called "truths" about money. Such as *money is the root of all evil* and *money doesn't grow on trees*.

In fact, those sayings aren't truths—rather, they're ingrained limiting beliefs.

Sure, evil people have done evil things with money, but money itself isn't inherently evil. From curing disease to providing shelter for your family to offering the pleasure of a home-cooked meal, there are countless examples of the positive effects of money.

It's true that money doesn't *literally* grow on trees, but the essence of scarcity that's conveyed by that expression is harmful to growth. Now's the time for you to rewrite your internal dialogue so that you can cultivate financial abundance.

In life, you can choose to lean toward either scarcity or abundance. Those with a Possible Mindset choose abundance.

Let's talk more about the difference between the two.

Stephen Covey, in his bestselling book *The 7 Habits of Highly*

Effective People, explains that a scarcity mindset frames the world in terms of what you *can't* have, whereas an abundance mindset sees the world in terms of what you *can* have. It's the difference between focusing on constraints versus opportunities.

But how do you make that mindset shift toward abundance? These four steps below will provide a road map:

1. **SET A SPECIFIC FINANCIAL GOAL**

   Start by asking yourself an open-ended question like "If I had all the money I needed and the time to spend it, what would I be doing?"

   How much money do you *actually* need to realize that vision?

   The key is to be specific. Write it down: _____

2. **TAKE STOCK OF YOUR ASSETS**

   Rather than let the scarcity mindset creep back in— listing the reasons why you *can't* create your dream scenario—start making a list of what resources you *do* have.

   For example, when Jenna and I had only $10,000, we could easily have thought, *There's no way we'll ever be able to raise $500,000 for our Grand Slam project.* Instead, we got creative, using an abundance mindset to ask ourselves how we could use what we had to raise more, which led to our building the website to attract sponsors.

   When I say "assets," I don't only mean your bank

balance. "Assets" in this case also refers to your experience, your education, your network, your work ethic, and whatever else is currently working in your favor.

Perhaps you want to travel abroad for a year, but your scarcity mindset tells you that the job market in your industry is supercompetitive and if you quit right now, you'll never be able to land as good of a job when you get back. An abundance mindset looks at this problem differently, viewing your ten years of experience as an asset, and trusts that when you return from your travels you'll be able to reenter the job market. The life lessons you gain from your travels may even land you a better career opportunity.

3. BE CLEAR ON YOUR *WHY*

Saying things like "I want to be rich" without a specific *why* rarely yields results. My *why* wasn't to have money just for the sake of filling my bank account. Rather, my passion for freedom, experiences, and impact fueled my desire to earn money.

What's your *why*? Try filling in the blank:

"I'm focused on earning more money so that I can . . .

. . . put my kids through college so they don't graduate with student debt

. . . have more freedom to pursue my hobbies and travel

. . . start a thriving nonprofit and give back to my community

. . . climb the Seven Summits . . .''

There's no right answer, but having a specific *why* that you truly believe in is crucial to generating abundance.

4. TAKE ACTION RELENTLESSLY

What I'm advocating isn't a get rich quick scheme. It's possible, likely even, that reaching your specific financial goal will take time. The key: don't give up.

Once you have your specific goal in mind, start working toward it every day. Visualize yourself achieving that outcome. Tell your friends and family about it. Take a small step, no matter how small, toward it every day.

Your action and daily belief will generate energy that'll help make your dreams a reality. Some people call this the Law of Attraction; others with a belief in forces greater than ourselves will say, "The Universe conspires to help." But there's nothing especially woo-woo about it. The fact is, if you're always scanning the horizon, you're more likely to catch sight of an opportunity.

Let me put it another way: when you start taking relentless action with an abundance mindset and a firm belief in a positive outcome, you'll give energy and oxygen to your specific goal and the specific *why* that links to it—and like-minded people who can help will be drawn to you. Before you know it, doors you never knew existed will open, presenting new resources and momentum for your vision.

KEY TAKEAWAY

Build *your* website, realize abundance
Your mindset has a significant influence on your bank account. Shifting from a scarcity mindset to an abundance mindset will go a long way toward helping you reach your financial goals. At the outset of your wealth-building journey, let go of your limiting beliefs around money, set a *specific* financial goal, take inventory of your assets, be clear on your *why*, and relentlessly pursue your goals with action.

HOW THIS APPLIES TO YOUR 12-HOUR WALK

Remember what my dad said, "The outdoors are free." The 12-Hour Walk is designed to cost practically nothing. As long as you have a pair of shoes and the will to make meaningful change, you have all that you need to reap the rewards of the 12-Hour Walk. The fact is, the majority of life's most valuable experiences cost little to nothing. As for your goals that *do* require money, use the time and space of the Walk to get clear on your specific objective and your *why*. Then adopt an abundance mindset—it will fuel your pursuits.

WITH A <u>POSSIBLE MINDSET</u>,

I believe that money is abundant and I can have it too.

Scan the QR code
or visit **12hourwalk.com/chapter11**
to view a short video that illuminates
the story from this chapter.

12

LIMITING BELIEF:

"I DON'T HAVE WHAT IT TAKES."

It is not the mountain we conquer, but ourselves.

—SIR EDMUND HILLARY

Some days sneak up on you like getting rear-ended by a car while you're parked at a stoplight. March 11, 2020, was one of those days for me.

I'd just returned home from my recently suspended book tour. My laptop was open on my knees and I was scrolling the day's headlines, trying to make sense of all that was happening.

BREAKING NEWS:

Trump Is Suspending Travel from
Europe to the United States—BuzzFeed

NBA Suspends Season After Player
Tests Positive for Coronavirus—NYTimes

Tom Hanks, Rita Wilson Say They've
Tested Positive for the Coronavirus—FoxNews

World Health Organization Declares
COVID-19 a Pandemic—TIME

"This is wild, look at this," I said to Jenna as I slid the computer across the couch. "I don't know, but I think it'll all blow over in a couple of weeks."

"I hope so," she replied, not bothering to look up from her phone. "Otherwise packing all that climbing gear for China was a giant waste of time." We'd spent the day packing ice axes, down suits, crampons, and 8000m climbing boots for our upcoming expedition.

A few minutes later, all hope was dashed.

"Colin! I don't think we'll be going to Everest . . ." Jenna burst out. "Go look at what *Outside* magazine just tweeted."

BREAKING NEWS:

China Just Closed the North Side of Mount Everest
—Outside Magazine

I covered my face with both of my hands, and for the first time began to accept that the world was forever changed.

▲ ▲ ▲

One year earlier, on a crisp spring day, Jenna and I had been walking our dog, Jack, near our house. The sun was out, but the winter snow still blanketed the Tetons like a white canvas draped over towering sculptures.

Nonchalantly, Jenna turned toward me and said, "I know I'm not really a climber, but do you think it'd be possible for me to climb Mount Everest one day?"

My eyes lit up. We'd climbed some peaks together over the years. We even got engaged at 19,000 feet on a mountaintop in Ecuador. Jenna had always been incredibly supportive of my adventures, but after witnessing firsthand the challenges and suffering I'd been through at the ends of the Earth and on mountaintops, she'd never shown much interest in personally taking on these kinds of larger expeditions.

"Are you serious?" I asked, beaming. She nodded back. "Then, heck yeah, it's possible. We'd have to train you up all year, but with the right mindset, you certainly have what it takes to reach the summit."

"Well, if I were to try, I'd want to climb from the Chinese side, the north side. I have no interest in the Nepal side. I'd never climb through the Khumbu Icefall," she stated emphatically. She was referencing an infamous section of Everest's south side route that had claimed the lives of many climbers.

"I get where you're coming from with the Khumbu Icefall," I said, recalling my climb through the terrifying ice maze when I'd summited Everest from Nepal in 2016. "The Chinese side sounds great to me—it'll be a new experience for both of us.

If you're committed to the goal, we can get you ready by next spring."

Commit she did.

For the next year, while still juggling all of the work with our businesses and helping me plan the Drake Passage row, Jenna trained for her goal of climbing Mount Everest. I taught her the necessary technical skills while we climbed several peaks together. She'd get up early and do laps on the mountains near our house, and when training outdoors wasn't an option she'd push herself through high-intensity gym routines.

She was *all* in, until that fateful day in March 2020, when in an instant it was *all* over.

▲ ▲ ▲

We relocated to the Oregon Coast for the total COVID lockdown that spring. Although it was a positive time in the sense that the 12-Hour Walk was born, overall it was a troubling time not just for us but the whole world. We quickly realized that the cancellation of our expedition was the least of our worries.

One gray Oregon day I found Jenna slumped in the TV room. "Let's refocus," I said. "Keep your training and fitness up. You'll get your shot on Everest next year when it opens up again."

"I've put a lot of thought into this, Colin, and given everything that's going on with COVID and the world, I honestly don't feel like training for Everest anymore. I'm over it."

I was unable to convince her to get back on the horse.

"I'm not going to climb Everest. It seems like a red flag that it didn't work out the first time for me—maybe it isn't meant to be. I'm not a climber anyway. And, frankly, I'd be humiliated if I tried and failed and we wasted all that money."

Sticking to her word, she stopped training completely.

▲ ▲ ▲

BREAKING NEWS:

Mount Everest to Reopen for First Climbers Post-Pandemic
—CNN

"Pass me those down mittens and that helmet, please," I said to Jenna, pointing at a pile of gear in our garage. It was March 11, 2021, exactly one year after COVID canceled our 2020 climbing plans, and the Everest season was officially back on.

I'd hardly had time to unpack my gear, having returned home from K2 only the month before. My heart was still aching. During those weeks at home I'd often found myself staring off into space, tears escaping my eyes, as I tried to make sense of the tragedy I'd just witnessed. Yet here I was, loading up my duffel bags again to return to the mountains.

"You sure you don't want to toss that in the bag just in case?" I asked, this time pointing to Jenna's down Everest summit suit, the one she'd bought before our planned expedition had been canceled the year prior.

"I'm sure," Jenna said with confidence. "I'm excited to come on the trek to Everest Base Camp with you, Colin, but I have no interest in climbing after the year we've been through."

China was still closed, but Nepal had recently opened its borders to climbers for the first time in a year. Our logistics operator, Arnold Coster, had generously agreed to credit the money we'd deposited to climb in China the year before if I wanted to climb this year in Nepal. We'd thought that deposit was long gone, but it turned out we had enough credit to fund one climber.

Since Jenna was no longer climbing, I decided that if I was going to return to Everest I should try something more challenging than my first climb in 2016. And so, I'd set the goal of attempting to become the first person to climb Mount Everest and then in one continuous push climb Lhotse—the fourth tallest mountain in the world—by traversing the shared ridgelines between both summits, *without* using supplemental oxygen.

After hours spent in the garage packing, I pulled a neatly folded stack of five flags off the shelf and placed them on the top of my duffel bag and zipped it closed. Each flag represented the home country of one of my five fallen friends on K2.

Jenna walked over to me and wrapped me in her arms, saying, "Bringing those flags up to the summit with you is a beautiful way to honor them. I'm proud of you. I hope you find some closure up there."

▲ ▲ ▲

A few days after we'd landed in Nepal and cleared the local COVID quarantine protocols, we boarded a helicopter, watching as the bustling streets of Kathmandu, full of mopeds and open air markets, disappeared into the distance. We figured we wouldn't be back to civilization for at least two months.

We spent the next week trekking through the majestic

Khumbu Valley surrounded by behemoth snowcapped mountains and passing ancient monasteries. Each day we planned to climb a couple thousand feet higher, beginning at 9,383 feet in the village of Lukla and steadily progressing toward Mount Everest Base Camp, located at 17,500 feet. By then, we hoped, our bodies would be pretty well adjusted to the thin air, though there'd be an intense stage of acclimatization even after that.

It felt like taking a step back in time a hundred years. There are no roads, just a narrow and steep footpath connecting the Sherpa villages of the Khumbu Valley.

Jenna stared in awe, eyes wide, breathing heavily. "I can hardly manage carrying my small backpack at this altitude," she said just as a villager bent over at his waist approached, carrying on his back several twenty-foot steel beams that had to weigh well over two hundred pounds. He cruised past us, flashing a friendly smile. Superhuman strength on full display.

We'd synced up our logistics so we could trek with Dr. Jon and our dear friend Mike Posner—the Grammy-nominated singer, songwriter, and record producer of "I Took a Pill in Ibiza" fame—who were climbing together. Posner brought a small guitar, and despite the physical strain of the trek, at night we relished the opportunity to sing songs, disconnect from devices, laugh, and tell stories over endless cups of tea.

It was a carefree time, but in the back of our minds, we knew the intensity and stakes that lay ahead.

On the seventh day of the trek, we crested a ridge high in the Khumbu Valley. For the first time we could see the fluorescent outline of the tents in Base Camp and make out the summit ridge of Everest in the distance, a glimmering titan towering over a landscape of legendary Himalayan peaks.

I'd teamed up with Dawa Finjhok Sherpa, a six-time Everest summiter, to help support my no-supplemental-oxygen ascent. Dawa and I had several mutual friends in the mountaineering community and I was excited that we'd be climbing together.

Dawa, with his kind eyes and confident demeanor, stood with his finger pointing toward the massive glacier above Everest Base Camp and in his accented English said, "See over there, Jenna, that's the infamous Khumbu Icefall. It can be scary climbing there, but I've seen how strong you are on the trek, you could climb it if you wanted."

Jenna politely smiled back, shaking her head. "I didn't train, Dawa. Base Camp is high enough for me. But I'm sure glad I made it here. Pictures don't do this place justice, the scale is otherworldly."

▲ ▲ ▲

Over the next week we settled into life at Base Camp and began the process of acclimatization. Before attempting to climb to the top of the world, I first needed to climb up and down the lower slopes to get my body prepared for the thin air in the mountain's highest reaches. There are four camps above Base Camp on the route to the summit, and I'd need to spend time at each of them.

It was a bitter cold and clear night. The full moon reflected off the snow, lighting up our view of the Khumbu Icefall from Base Camp. Wrapped in our puffy down jackets, beanies pulled tight over our heads, Jenna and I stared out at a row of headlamps zigzagging through the Icefall. Another climbing team was making a rotation up the mountain.

"You know," I said, "Dawa is right. You could climb up the Icefall if you wanted. You're plenty strong. Your permit allows you to go as high as Camp 2." Smiling and looking up toward the night sky, I continued, "And besides you think *this* view is good? The view from above the Icefall is beyond words."

Jenna sighed. "I can't stop thinking about the sixteen Sherpas who died in the Icefall avalanche in 2014. I don't want to die up there," she said. "But I've been staring at the mountain all week wondering what it must be like. I don't want to live with regrets." I could see her mind working through her dilemma, but I stayed quiet not wanting to interrupt her stream of consciousness.

After a couple of minutes gazing into the canopy of stars, she spoke again. "Okay, fine. I'll go up with you guys next time, as long as you and Dawa promise to keep me safe."

"I promise," I whispered, kissing her, thrilled about this new development.

▲ ▲ ▲

The three of us woke up at midnight to climb through the Khumbu Icefall—a dizzying maze of vertical ice and crevasses—hoping the cold of night would make the precarious ice more stable.

Out of the darkness ahead of us came an ominous sound. "What's that, Colin?" Jenna asked, startled. I shined my headlamp in her direction and could make out a worried look on her face.

"It's the ice creaking and moving. We've got to move quickly through here—it can all collapse on us at any moment."

Then came the ladders.

In front of us was a crevasse with a sheer drop-off into a seemingly bottomless dark hole. The only way across? An icy tightrope act over rickety aluminum ladders roped together to form a makeshift bridge.

Jenna stepped onto the first of a series of such ladders that spanned the deepest and most dangerous crevasses on the route. I could hear her steel crampons scraping against the rungs of the ladder. Each step now had potentially life-or-death consequences.

"Trust your feet. You've got this," I said, trying to calmly assure her, despite my terrible habit of picturing our bodies hanging there limp if the ladder dislodged while we were crossing.

Her movements were understandably tentative, stepping out over this two-hundred-foot icy abyss, but she never let her nerves stop her. She climbed with a fearless tenacity through the night.

As the sun rose, we jumped over the final crevasse of the Khumbu Icefall, and later that day arrived to Camp 2 at 21,500 feet. Mount Everest's summit was still towering over a mile above our heads, and Lhotse, my other objective, stood right in front of us guarded by a 5,000-foot near vertical wall of ice.

▲ ▲ ▲

The following morning Dawa and I left to spend two nights higher on the mountain, at Camp 3, and during that stay we touched Camp 4 in the "Death Zone"—an altitude above 26,000 feet where the human body is slowly dying.

Jenna's permit prohibited her from climbing any higher. Even though she'd shown nothing but strength in getting to Camp 2, I was worried about leaving her alone for a couple of days. She'd never been above 21,000 feet, and I couldn't shake the reality of what extreme altitude did to people. Up that high, it's all too common for climbers to get altitude sickness, have trouble eating and sleeping, and mentally break down.

Thankfully, when I returned to Camp 2, I found Jenna healthy and in high spirits.

"I've had a great couple of days here, just looking up at Everest," she said. "What a stunning place. Maybe one day we can come back, and I can climb to the summit?" She had a glint in her eye that I'd never seen before, as if she'd been hypnotized by the splendor of her surroundings.

"I've always known you have what it takes to climb this mountain."

"One day . . ." Her voice trailed off as we packed up our gear to head back down to Base Camp to rest.

Our bodies acclimatized now, Dawa and I would wait for ideal weather to make our summit push.

▲ ▲ ▲

What was supposed to be a few days' stay at Base Camp turned into a two-week ultramarathon of patience as Everest got unexpectedly battered by back-to-back cyclones. During this time we received the tragic news of an American and a Swiss climber who both died during a summit attempt.

Jenna and I took a walk to clear our heads and stretch our

legs, which had begun to feel like Jell-O after all the waiting around.

A disheveled, visibly exhausted climber with a wind-chapped face crossed our path. "There's too much snow. It's too windy up high; we're packing up and getting the hell out of here," he said, shuffling past us.

Passing by other camps, we watched in sinking disappointment as team after team was making the same choice to abandon their expedition, based on the poor forecast and escalating COVID risk in Base Camp.

"I'm not ready to give up. I think I'll still get a shot," I said to Jenna and to myself, grasping for optimism and hoping I'd get the weather window I'd need for a summit push.

"What if one day was today?" Jenna asked, a seeming non sequitur.

I looked back confused, "What?"

"I guess what I'm trying to say is, I know I don't have a summit permit. I know the season is almost over. I know I didn't pack my down suit. I know there's a high chance I'll fail if I try, but I can't shake this feeling. I'm all the way over here, now, and I don't know if I'll ever make it back. Do you think there's any way I could go for the summit?"

I stopped dead in my tracks. "I've been secretly hoping you'd say that."

I could feel a flood of excitement as I pulled Jenna into my arms. I continued, "I care about my no oxygen project, but truthfully the main reason I wanted to come back here was to share the experience with you, like we'd planned last year. I'm certain we can ask around and find an extra down suit for you. On the other hand, I have no idea if we can get a permit and sort out logistics this late, but I'll inquire around Base Camp. Nothing would make me happier than standing on the top of the world with you. We'd have an unbelievable story to tell our grandkids one day."

▲ ▲ ▲

Two days later we awoke to the thunderous sound of helicopter rotor blades, followed by an unfamiliar foreign voice asking, "Miss Jenna? Miss Jenna? Is there a Miss Jenna here?"

I unzipped our tent and popped my head outside to find a Nepali man carrying a briefcase with tape on the outside that read *Nepal Ministry of Tourism*. Sure enough, a Nepali friend at Base Camp had pulled off a miracle. The man opened the briefcase and handed Jenna a pen. "Just sign here and you have an official Everest permit," he said, laughing. "Latest permit we've ever issued, I think."

Jenna looked at me and laughed nervously. "I'm not telling my mom until we're back down here safely."

Problems solved. Time to climb.

▲ ▲ ▲

We took a gamble on the weather as we climbed again through the Khumbu Icefall, this time during a mounting blizzard. Tracking the forecast, I saw what looked like the final summit weather window of the season approaching in a few days, but the only way to be high enough on the mountain to take advantage of it was to risk a trip through the Icefall in deteriorating conditions.

Our goggles were strapped on and hoods pulled up tight as the headwind pelted us with snow. We were walking blind. In the furious snowy static I could only roughly make out Jenna, who was just a few feet away. Through the whiteout, we gingerly navigated the labyrinth of crevasses and ladders, praying for safe passage.

Mercifully, after twelve hours battling this unrelenting storm, we spotted the orange fabric of our tent in Camp 2 and climbed inside, collapsing from exhaustion.

I could hardly hear myself think over the incessant rattling of our tent poles.

"I've got to go to the bathroom," Jenna announced.

"Be careful," I shouted, poking my head out the tent door as Jenna exited into the tempest.

Just then a sixty-mile-per-hour gust blasted us, and I helplessly watched as Jenna was knocked off her feet and tossed into a nearby snowbank.

She crawled back inside, making a futile attempt to dust off all the snow, and then burrowed deep into her sleeping bag, covering all but her nose with the layers of down—just enough to breathe. "Colin, I'm not sure I've ever been more uncomfortable. The view from the top had better be worth it," she mumbled.

I grinned, thinking about the 1s and 10s.

Two nights later, as the forecast had predicted, the wind finally calmed and everything quieted, like a faucet when you turn off the water. We were sleeping head to toe, the only way to comfortably fit inside our claustrophobic tent. I sat up and kissed Jenna on the forehead. "Get some good sleep tonight, we'll leave first thing in the morning for Camp 3, and then the following night for the summit!"

Crash, bang. "Heeeeelllp!" I awoke to Jenna screaming at the top of her lungs.

Like a waking nightmare, our tent was caving in on top of us, and the deafening sounds of a freight train barreling past filled our ears. Disoriented, I tried to sit up, pushing against the roof of our now dismembered tent, trying to make sense of what was happening.

Jenna's head was stuck beneath the uphill side of the collapsed tent. I felt an adrenaline surge, my brain finally processing the dire circumstances.

"It's an avalanche!" I shouted, grabbing Jenna's body and dislodging her head from the snowbank that had smashed into our tent.

Silence.

As fast as it had come, it passed. Several climbers from other teams were scurrying around, surveying the damage through the glow of their headlamps. I found Dawa digging out a tent. "We're very lucky I think, Colin, we only got hit by the edge of the avalanche, no major injuries, just a bunch of butchered tents. Try to go to sleep if you can, let's talk about a plan in the morning."

We managed to reerect our tent in a makeshift way for the night, but sleep was nearly impossible after that rush of adrenaline.

As the sun rose, Jenna sat up, her face puffy from the altitude and fatigue. "Camp 2 sucks, let's get the hell out of here."

215

"Yeah," I agreed, resigned to the inevitable. "Let's eat breakfast, and then we can climb down to Base Camp and go home."

"Down?" she said with a confused tone, "I mean, I'm definitely not staying here, but I didn't come this far to only come *this* far. If it's safe to keep climbing, we're going up!"

▲ ▲ ▲

As we climbed up to Camp 3 we were greeted by sunshine and stillness, leaving the wreckage of snapped tent poles and ripped fabric behind.

Perched on a precarious icy ledge, barely larger than the width of our tent, we fell asleep that night, trying to block out the knowledge that if we got hit by an avalanche on this tiny platform there'd be no surviving it.

Thankfully, the night passed uneventfully, and we continued our ascent that next morning to 26,000 feet.

Camp 4 is the final camp before the summit, an unforgiving wasteland that we planned to use only as a temporary rest stop for a few hours. Our intent had been to arrive at midday and depart at sundown—climbing through the entire night to hopefully reach the summit the following morning. Even though I'd been to Camp 4 several times before, there's no getting used to the vulnerable feeling of the Death Zone. There's little hope of rescue if anything goes wrong up there. The feeling is like how I imagine an astronaut must feel when they're floating outside the International Space Station during a spacewalk.

Despite the setting, Jenna didn't show any sign of nerves.

Instead, her insecurity and nervousness had been replaced by a calm confidence.

"How are you feeling? Ready for the summit push?" I asked her as we huddled in our wind-battered tent at Camp 4, making final adjustments to our oxygen masks and gear. I'd happily given up my no-supplemental-oxygen Everest-Lhotse attempt so that I'd be as lucid and focused as possible to support Jenna's climb.

Jenna looked like the Marshmallow Man in her borrowed bright orange down suit. She smiled back. "I know I didn't train properly for this, and I'm sure people will criticize me, but honestly, my body feels strong. Most important, my mind feels strong. Let's go to the summit," she said, grabbing her backpack and stepping out of our tent into the windy night.

▲ ▲ ▲

One step. Rest. Three breaths.

Two steps. Rest. Five breaths.

Every step is hard-earned on an Everest summit push. We expected the final push to take at least twelve hours. Dawa led the way, followed by Jenna and then me. I kept a watchful eye as Jenna made deliberate steps up the steep snow slopes through the darkness. It was minus-thirty degrees out and a steady wind was blowing from our left side. We kept our hoods up to block the gusts and try to stave off frostbite.

The long night passed in a delirium of headlamp glow and oxygen-deprived thoughts as we inched our way higher on the mountain.

"Take your hood down for a second and look to your right," I shouted, pointing off to the east.

The first glow of sunrise was lighting up the horizon framed by a sheer two-vertical-mile drop-off on either side of us.

Jenna's crampons dug into the steep snow as she peered out at the burnt orange horizon. With a few more labored steps we crested the South Summit, a tiny flat perch with unobstructed views of the final knife-edge, rocky ridgeline that led to the true summit.

We took a seat on this vertigo-inducing platform for a few moments to steady our nerves and drink in the splendor of the moment. There were only a couple dozen other climbers spread out on the route that morning, and it felt like we had the mountain all to ourselves.

"We're close," I said, putting my arm around Jenna's shoulders. "But this last part is going to be difficult, we need to stay focused." Not offering more than I needed to, both of us knowing this final stretch to the top had claimed the lives of many climbers.

The wind had picked up quite violently, but there was no chance we'd turn back now. Jenna stood up with determination.

"Let's finish this," she said, pulling her hood up tight around her face. She concentrated on forward progress, her intuition telling her to tune out the dizzying drop-offs and focus on just the step in front of her.

The final ridge was an obstacle course of jagged rock formations and steep ice and snow that required gymnast-like dexterity and balance to navigate. Perhaps at sea level the terrain would have been easier to climb, but at this altitude, the simplest movements felt nearly impossible.

Jenna pulled with all her strength to climb over the last steep rock ledge. We gazed up and saw the Tibetan prayer flags just ahead that marked our destination.

"Top of the world!" I shouted, as we took our final steps to the summit. I held Jenna as tight as I could in my arms, our smiles stretching as wide as the limitless horizon around us.

Jenna lowered her ice-covered mask. "I can't believe it. I did it. We did it! I love you," she said through heavy breaths and tears.

I took off my goggles so she could see my eyes clearly. "Jenna, I've witnessed some incredible feats throughout my athletic career, but what you just accomplished is unparalleled in my book. It's a true testament to the power of your mind."

She kissed my frozen lips as Dawa snapped a few summit photos.

I reached into my backpack and raised up the country flags of the five friends I'd lost on K2, saying each of their names aloud.

"I know you've all been on this mountain before. I miss you. I love you," I said, staring up at the sky, imagining them all smiling down on us.

▲ ▲ ▲

We stayed on the summit only a few moments longer, battered by the fierce wind. Years of dreaming and struggling boiled down to a handful of minutes. Getting down safely with all our fingers and toes was the true definition of success on Everest.

As we put on our packs and turned to go down, Jenna spoke over the wind, "There were so many times the past couple of years I never thought I'd be here. Thank you for believing in me every step of the way."

I leaned over and whispered in her ear, "It's been one hell of an adventure. I'm so proud of you. What do you say we go on an even greater adventure?"

She looked back at me confused.

"Let's go home and start a family!" I cried out.

She wrapped me tight in her arms, joyful tears flowing again as we climbed down to begin our next adventure.

There was nothing I wanted more.

HOW THIS STORY APPLIES TO YOU

Now that was a 10!

Despite there not being a world record or a medal for standing on that summit, sharing this once-in-a-lifetime moment on the top of the world with my wife—beaming at her with pride—exceeded the satisfaction I'd experienced on all my previous adventures combined.

In that moment, Jenna became the 89th American woman—and the 676th woman in history—to summit Mount Everest.

So what does Jenna's story teach about how you can reach the summit of your own Mount Everest?

First, you don't have to be an "expert" to achieve great things. Second, use the power of incremental goal setting—if you can take one step farther and aim one camp higher, before you know it you'll arrive at the top. Perhaps most important, understand that the path to success is unlikely to be linear, and that getting where you want to go will almost always entail overcoming multiple limiting beliefs.

Each of the previous chapters focused on a single limiting belief so that you have the tools to overcome any given one when it arises. But Jenna's experience shows us the reality: limiting beliefs rarely travel alone. Rather, they tend to crowd together, so you need to be equipped to identify and overcome many simultaneously.

If you're at least my age, you probably remember playing that old arcade game Whac-A-Mole. Each time one of the moles popped up, you took your black mallet and knocked it down. Inevitably, before you knew it, another mole would spring back.

Battling our limiting beliefs is just like that. Identifying and overcoming real-life Whac-A-Moles is, foundationally, all about mental strength—about developing a Possible Mindset.

But how do we do that?

The most important muscle any of us has is the six inches between our ears.

I use the word *muscle* very intentionally here. Intuitively we know that if we want to strengthen our biceps, we need to hit the gym and lift weights. Unfortunately, even though the same principle holds for our minds, we rarely act on it. Rather, we relax in the zone of comfortable complacency and let our mental muscle atrophy.

To increase the strength of your mind, it's essential that you take it to the gym, do your reps on the mental bench press. Unlocking your best life depends on it.

Which brings us back to the 12-Hour Walk. On its surface the Walk may seem like an exercise for your calves, quads, and glute muscles. But it's not. The 12-Hour Walk is meant to exercise the most important muscle you have: your mind.

By committing to this challenge, you'll jump-start your mind—jolt it into purposeful activity. I like to think of this adventure as a walking meditation—one that will crystalize all of the lessons in this book. By investing one day in your mental training, you'll be able to springboard into your future equipped with a Possible Mindset to overcome life's largest obstacles.

If someone asks you why you're taking on this 12-Hour Walk, your answer is simple: "I'm training my mind."

Just as I was thrilled to show Jenna the view from Everest's summit—to see her fully exhibit a Possible Mindset—I'm excited to think of the person *you'll* be when you return from the 12-Hour Walk. Prepare to meet a new, more confident you.

The time is now to leave the comfort zone of your couch and swap your slippers for sneakers. Get ready to learn how to embrace the 1s and relish the 10s that most people will never get to experience.

Your Possible Mindset will remind you that you're a "rower" or whatever it is you want to be. You're not an imposter, so claim your identity. Know that there's both ample time and also an abundance of money to help you achieve anything you desire.

As you step into the arena, there'll be some blood, sweat, and tears—and maybe if it's the dead of winter when you're taking your Walk, some frozen tears. But you'll soon understand that "it's not the critic who counts," especially when you're backed by a supportive community. Just make sure to steer clear of crabs.

You now know that there's really no such thing as failure. The only failure is in not trying. As your fear of failure melts away, you'll keep persevering no matter what happens, until the equation snaps into place: Failure + Perseverance = Success.

When you opened *The 12-Hour Walk*, you likely felt some apprehension. You wondered if this challenge was really within your reach. Since you're still reading, it shows that your answer is yes. It's safe to say it's no longer a hard call—there are no more pros and cons to weigh.

Your intuition is your guiding force. Trust it.

KEY TAKEAWAY

Make "one day" today

It's easy to put off living your best life now, allowing limiting beliefs to get in the way of taking immediate action. We can always find reasons to mortgage the present for the future—to deceive ourselves with the story that *one day* we'll retire and travel, *one day* we'll find the time to pursue our dreams, *one day* we'll climb our Mount Everest. But as Jenna realized, standing at the base of that Himalayan behemoth, there's nothing stopping you from making "one day" today.

HOW THIS APPLIES TO YOUR 12-HOUR WALK

The 12-Hour Walk is a stand-in for your Everest. When you commit to it, you'll need to face and overcome the limiting beliefs that have been holding you back. By completing the Walk, you'll have forged a Possible Mindset and be equipped to climb any Everest you desire.

WITH A <u>POSSIBLE MINDSET</u>,

I have what it takes to climb *my* Everest.

Scan the QR code
or visit **12hourwalk.com/chapter12**
to view a short video that illuminates
the story from this chapter.

PART III

COMMIT

EPILOGUE

All truly great thoughts are conceived while walking.

—FRIEDRICH NIETZSCHE

You didn't think I was going to leave you hanging, did you?

I started this book with a question:

"What's *your* Everest?"

As your guide, it seems only fair that I answer that question myself.

I fully expect to climb many more mountains and continue to take on adventures in remote corners of the world. Those adventures light me up, teach me, provide purpose and deep fulfillment, and always remind me what matters most.

And yet my next Everest may *not* be what you'd have guessed. Coincidentally, though, it's something you can play a major part in.

So here goes: *my* Everest is to inspire ten million people to complete the 12-Hour Walk.

A world where that occurs—now, that's one I aspire to live in. It's a world full of people living their best lives—filled with purpose, community, empathy, love, and courage. It's a world where "the mass of men" (all humankind) sing their songs while rising above "lives of quiet desperation."

So what do you say? Are you ready to overcome the limiting beliefs that are holding you back and unlock your Possible Mindset?

The time for sharing my stories has come to an end. Now it's time for you to author the next chapter of *your* unique story.

Don't worry, you're not alone. I'll still be here to guide you, and there's a global community of 12-Hour Walkers ready to support you. Embrace the adventure ahead.

Just don't overthink it. Scan the final QR code or visit the link 12hourwalk.com/commit and put the Walk on your calendar today. The longer you wait, the less likely you are to use the momentum of this moment to initiate lasting positive change.

Fight back against those limiting beliefs that are popping up.

Invest one day. Your best life awaits.

TAKE YOUR FIRST STEP RIGHT NOW AND COMMIT TO

the 12HOURWALK

Scan the QR code
or visit **12hourwalk.com/commit**
to sign up for the Walk and
unlock your best life.

APPENDIX

THE 12-HOUR WALK

INSTRUCTIONS:

1. **COMMIT**—Pick a day on your calendar to complete the 12-Hour Walk by visiting: **12hourwalk.com/commit.**

2. **RECORD**—Before you set out on your walk, record a short video of yourself to verbalize your intentions. What limiting beliefs do you want to silence? Describe how you hope to feel when you complete the 12-Hour Walk.

3. **UNPLUG**—Turn your phone on airplane mode before starting your 12-Hour Walk. The 12-Hour Walk is designed to be taken alone, with no external inputs— no companions, no headphones, no podcasts, no music, no email, no texts, no social media—for the entire twelve hours. Keep your phone with you for safety, but use it only to record a quick video or write a note to reflect on later.

4. **WALK**—Begin your 12-Hour Walk. Just like life, you choose the destination. Remain outside for twelve hours, walking in silence. The setting you're walking in doesn't need to be completely silent, but you do. Maintaining *your* silence is the key. Ambient city noise is okay.

5. **REST**—The 12-Hour Walk isn't a race. Take as many breaks as you need. It doesn't matter if you walk one mile or fifty; as long as you keep moving when you can, you're winning.

6. **REFLECT**—Record a video as you finish your 12-Hour Walk. Ask yourself: How do you feel? What did you discover? What limiting beliefs did you overcome? What do you now feel capable of with your Possible Mindset?

POSSIBLE MINDSET™

an empowered way of thinking that unlocks a life of limitless possibilities.

WITH A <u>POSSIBLE MINDSET</u>, I . . .

. . . love stepping out of my comfort zone because it leads to fulfillment.

. . . can learn, grow, and become anything.

. . . can heal, even if I've been broken. I can stand back up, even if I've been knocked down.

. . . can dare greatly, even when facing potential criticism.

. . . know that failures are the foundation of my success—winners lose the most.

. . . trust my gut. I *do* know the answer.

. . . have the power to choose friends who'll help me become the best version of myself.

. . . have enough time and I spend it wisely.

. . . believe that money is abundant and I can have it too.

. . . have what it takes to climb *my* Everest.

#12HourWalk #BePossible

FREQUENTLY ASKED QUESTIONS

What if I don't know what my Everest is?
If you're struggling to answer the question "What's my Everest?"—because maybe you don't have a specific vision or goal at the front of your mind right now—you can still use the 12-Hour Walk to cultivate a Possible Mindset, which will be highly beneficial in whatever you ultimately choose to pursue.

Use your 12-Hour Walk experience as an opportunity to ponder. In walking out the front door, your intention can be *My Everest is to discover what my Everest is so I can live my best life pursuing it.*

Do I need to train for the 12-Hour Walk?
The short answer is: No.

The 12-Hour Walk is meant to meet you exactly where you're at today. It's not a race. There's no extra credit handed out for going farther or faster. Listen to your body and take as many breaks as you need throughout the day. The goal isn't to injure yourself.

It doesn't matter if you walk one mile or fifty, as long as you set aside the full twelve hours and walk as much as you can while maintaining your silence. Do that and you'll reap the benefits of completing the Walk.

Will this test you physically? Yes. But as I taught you earlier, the 12-Hour Walk is really about training your mind.

What are important safety essentials?

Safety is of the utmost priority on the Walk.

A few tips:

- ▶ Wear brightly colored clothing.
- ▶ Bring a headlamp and spare batteries.
- ▶ Bring your phone but keep it on airplane mode. Use it only in case of emergency.
- ▶ Tell a family member or friend your general planned route and projected return time.
- ▶ Carry some spare cash, just in case.
- ▶ Avoid highly trafficked roads with no shoulder. Sidewalks and trails are the safest options.
- ▶ If you're walking on a road without a sidewalk, walk on the left side—if you're in a country where motorists drive on the right—so you can see oncoming cars. The opposite is true in the UK, Australia, or other left-side-driving countries.

Do I have to leave from my house or can I walk somewhere else?

I highly recommend starting from your front door and walking nearby your home. It's more grounding and will help you implement your Possible Mindset into your daily life.

The 12-Hour Walk is designed to be as accessible as possible. There are no set requirements regarding where you choose to walk. Don't let waiting to be on a vacation in a picturesque location be the excuse for not putting your Walk on the calendar now.

Can I walk in a city with noise and other pedestrians?
If you live in a bustling city, that's okay, the Walk doesn't require a rural or remote setting. City noise and passing pedestrians don't negate your personal commitment to solitude and silence. As long as you're walking alone without actively engaging with others, you're upholding the guidelines.

Do you have additional questions for me, like:

- ▶ "What's the best footwear for the 12-Hour Walk?"
- ▶ "What nutrition do you recommend for fueling my day?"
- ▶ "Where do I go to the bathroom?"
- ▶ "Can I walk with someone else or does this have to be completed alone?"
- ▶ "Can I bring my dog or pet with me?"
- ▶ "Is the 12-Hour Walk something I can do more than once?"

For answers to these additional questions and many more resources, visit: **12hourwalk.com**.

ACKNOWLEDGMENTS

Jenna B, the love of my life. Thank you for your never-ending support. I'm deeply grateful to walk beside you as your partner in life and business. You inspire me daily with your strength, wisdom, and creativity. The 12-Hour Walk wouldn't be what it is without all the time and dedication you've spent on this idea. Thank you for staying up so many late nights, reading drafts, editing passages, and improving the book page by page, not to mention your steadfast vision for the cover design. Infinite love, my dear—here's to continuing to add chapters to our love story.

Blake Brinker, my ride or die. You're a true creative master. Any person hoping to bring a big idea into the world would be lucky to have you in their corner. It's been a true honor to work with you to nurture this idea—the 12-Hour Walk—from inception to fruition. Not only are you one of my dearest friends, but also one of my greatest teachers. I'm eternally grateful for our many collaborations over the years, and I look forward to many more days playing in the "control booth" together. Thanks for being the initial willing test subject for the Walk. I hope millions will ultimately complete it, but you will always be the first!

A special thanks to Sarah Passick and Celeste Fine, my incomparable literary agents. I'm grateful for your trust in my ideas and for helping me transform them into books. It's a great pleasure to work with you. Thank you to the entire team at Park & Fine Literary and Media.

Thank you to the whole publishing team at Scribner and Simon & Schuster. In particular, my editor, Rick Horgan, and publisher, Nan Graham. Thank you to Jon Karp for championing my work from day one. It has been a pleasure to bring multiple books into the world with you all.

Additional thanks to Ali Rogers for your video-editing genius and your help in developing the QR code content. To the Luum Studio team and my dear friend Paul Tannenbaum for building the digital ecosystem for the 12-Hour Walk. To Dan Paiser for your early contributions to the manuscript. And to my inner circle group of advance readers and test walkers for helping me to improve this concept:

Donna Besaw, Danielle Bloch, Eileen Brady, David Brinker, Henry Cadwalader, Matt Chandler, Drew Christopher, Lucas Clarke, Kelly Cooper, Eric Eriksen, Lindsey Fielding, Lynn Greico, Marc Hodulich, Daniel Jeydel, Nate Keating, Sadie Morrison, Alejandro Navia, Tim O'Connor, Ali Rogers, Brian Rohter, Laurie Skalla, Marc Skalla, Andrew Spaulding, Danielle Spaulding, David Spaulding, and Caleb Spaulding.

Last, I want to thank *you*, the reader. This book was written for you. Thank you for your trust and your courage in taking on the 12-Hour Walk. I can't wait to see what you accomplish with your Possible Mindset.

#BePossible

ABOUT THE AUTHOR

COLIN O'BRADY is a ten-time world record–breaking explorer, *New York Times* bestselling author of *The Impossible First*, speaker, entrepreneur, and expert on mindset.

Colin's highly publicized expeditions have been followed by millions and his work has been featured in the *New York Times* and *Forbes* and on *The Tonight Show*, the BBC, *The Joe Rogan Experience*, and NBC's *Today*. His feats include the world's first solo, unsupported, and fully human-powered crossing of Antarctica; speed records for the Explorers Grand Slam and the Seven Summits; and the world's first human-powered ocean row across the Drake Passage.

He regularly speaks at Fortune 100 companies such as Nike, Google, and Amazon and at top universities including Harvard, Yale, and UPenn. He's also the co-founder of 29029 Everesting.

Native to the Pacific Northwest, he now lives in Jackson Hole, Wyoming, with his wife, Jenna Besaw, and dog, Jack. Engage with Colin @colinobrady or at colinobrady.com.

Visit 12hourwalk.com and IG @12hourwalk, and download the 12HourWalk app to join the movement.